"A stranger is just a friend you haven't met yet"

After my girlfriend Ashlin got accepted into Vet School and I quit my job in April 2015, we decided to say our final goodbyes to the city that never sleeps and got ready for a new challenge before we finally moved to California. In two months we cycled across the US from Yorktown, VA to San Diego. The journey took us through ten states covering more than 3,500 miles and our bikes were loaded with 40lbs each. We camped along the way as well as stayed in motels or various cyclist friendly lodgings such as churches or fire departments. We saw the beauty of this country by bike and made new connections with the people we met along the way. Why?

That's a question which we were asked a lot. We couldn't give satisfying answers except that we were looking for a new adventure and said it would make us happy. Happiness leads to success and not the other way around. In today's world, we find ourselves struggling to focus on happy things. With the media highlighting terror, war and natural disasters, we simply forgot how many happy things surround us. This trip was supposed to show us and the people around us, how many good things are still happening everyday, even in the most remote areas of the United States.

We didn't train at all but we planned ahead by reading stories and blogs of other TransAm cyclists. The Adventure Cycling Association Maps guided us through the first two thirds of our trip but the rest were self-planned routes. When we started, we didn't know if we could handle 60 miles a day or only 40. It was a learning curve and we enjoyed moving it up everyday.

During our two months on the road, I wrote a daily blog which I transformed into this book.

This is our story.

This is our adventure.

Enjoy reading it and look for the hidden flip book feature.

Day 0 – Heading to Yorktown

We left New York with mixed feelings after spending 4 ½ and 6 ½ years in this city, respectively.

It's an incredible moment when you leave a place with nothing more than two bicycles and four panniers with all your stuff for the next two months.

The journey down to Yorktown, VA took us through Washington DC and the blooming forests of Virginia which we will pass again once we are on our trip tomorrow.

Yorktown, Williamsburg and Jamestown build the Historic Triangle and are all cities we will pass on our first day of cycling. They mark important historic places which include the first lasting settlement Jamestown and the battlefield of Yorktown where in 1781, the Continental Army defeated British General Cornwallis and his Redcoats in the last great engagement of the war for independence.

We are looking forward to the next two months with camping etc. but tonight we are going to enjoy the amenities of a motel to start fresh into our first day of cycling.

Life is good.

Day 1 - Westbound and down

....loaded up and truckin', we're gonna do what they say can't be done. We've got a long way to go and a short time to get there. I'm west bound, just watch ol' "Bandit" run.

Those are the starting lines of one of my favorite songs from the movie "Smokey and the Bandit" (I replaced east with west) and when I started playing this Jerry Reed song today after ~50 miles it gave us a push for the last stretch of a 63 mile ride. Actually it has been 67 miles since we had to cycle from our motel to the official TransAm starting point in Yorktown.
Here we put the rear tires of our bicycles into the water. Now it will only be 3,500 miles until we can do the same with the front tires in the Pacific Ocean. The Tire Dipping Ceremony is one of many traditions among TransAm cyclists and we are looking forward to complete it once we arrive in San Diego.
The departure from Yorktown was very easy and exciting. We only had to follow the Colonial Parkway which brought us directly to Williamsburg. Williamsburg was also the place of our first coffee break and the place where we met our first fellow TransAm riders Cindy and Rob (www.campingtandem.blogspot.com) who had the coolest Cannondale Tandem I have ever seen (see pic below). From there we rode our Treks to Jamestown where we got on a bike trail which brought us almost to the end. We only had to go back on the highway for the last 5-6 miles where the shoulder was narrow and a few trucks passed us. Fortunately, most all of the passing cars and trucks slowed down and gave us a lot of space.
63 miles later, we finally arrived at Willis Church. There couldn't have been a better place to stop. We were welcomed by pastor Mark who gave us a tour and showed

us showers, kitchen, sleeping areas and also gave us the Wi-Fi code. It's mind-blowing how much friendliness we received and we are so thankful that we can spend the night here all by ourselves.

We haven't decided on our final stop for tomorrow night. It could be the fire department in Mineral, which would mean a 70 mile ride, or finding a place in Ashland after ~40 miles. We will decide tomorrow depending on how we feel. For now, we say goodnight!

Day 2 – We are on Fire

At least that's how our legs felt after the rolling hills of Virginia. Fortunately, we are staying at a place where people know how to deal with fire. The Mineral Volunteer Fire Department.

Today's 1700 ft. elevation gain was definitely a big challenge but it was actually one of the days with the lowest elevation gain considering our further stages. The bicycle route 76 took us from Willis Church via Mechanicsville to Ashland where many cyclists stop for a lunch, coffee or dinner break. The food is really good and they even have a guestbook for cyclists to write down their contact details. After a quick stop at the local bike shop, we discussed the upcoming miles and decided to take a shorter route from Bumpass to Mineral which saved us five miles and a lot of unnecessary hills. We couldn't have planned it better because once we arrived in Mineral the rain clouds, which followed us throughout the whole day, poured water all over Mineral.

The firefighters welcomed us, showed us around and soon we were on our way to load up on some carbs. Mineral is pretty small but luckily a good Mexican restaurant is right across the street. With stomachs full of chips and salsa, burritos, carnitas and dessert we should be refueled for the next day.

Tomorrow we will ride a little less than the last two days and should arrive after 54 miles in Charlottesville, VA. However, elevation gain should be even a little more than today.

Day 3 – „Y'all gettin' a little wet today, huh? "

This was probably the best Virginia accent sentence we heard on this rainy day today and to be honest, I love it. It happened at a gas station halfway on our trip to Charlottesville, VA which was supposed to be 54 miles but after talking to a local guy and checking Google Maps for the best bicycle route from Mineral to Charlottesville, we decided to cycle off the Transamerica trail on the SR250 which saved us at least ten miles or one hour of cycling. The shoulder got a little narrow from time to time but traffic wasn't so heavy.

We eventually arrived in Charlottesville, home of University of Virginia. On our way we tried to arrange our first Warm Showers stay. Warm Showers lists the contact details of cyclists or fans of cycling who are offering a place to stay. After a couple of no's, we were almost about to give up but found Ross' and his fiancée's profile. They invited us to stay at their house and we couldn't have asked for a better first Warm Shower host. Ross is a returned Peace Corps Volunteer from Cape Verde and did a lot of bicycle touring in his past. His fiancée Mary spent a long time in Haiti and is about to graduate from grad school soon. Ross made vegan tacos for us and we brought a nice growler of beer from the brewery around the corner. We kept talking forever and also got to snuggle with their dog and cat. Now we are ready for bed and excited for our upcoming trip to Afton tomorrow. Life is good and hope y'all are havin' a good night.

Day 4 – Cookie Lady NO – Gingerbread Lady YES

 Day 4 started with sunshine and nice temperatures in Charlottesville. After a great night at Ross and Mary's place we headed to Bodo's Bagel for breakfast. If you decide to have breakfast in Charlottesville, you should definitely go there. It seems like it's THE place to be. Since we had only 29 miles planned we took it very slow and enjoyed our bagels at The Tog which is basically a park close to the university campus.

We decided to follow the Adventure Cycling maps today and were directed off the main roads and ended up in one of the most beautiful parts of Charlottesville and Virginia. I guess you could call it the Malibu of Charlottesville which is halfway to Crozet. Traffic was almost non-existent so we finally got to shoot some GoPro pictures which you can see below. After Crozet the hills got a lot steeper and we went up to 2,000ft elevation to Afton, VA – home of the famous Cookie Lady who unfortunately passed away in 2012. People still take care of her house and cyclists are still allowed to stay there but since we never heard back from them we tried Warm Showers again and got a response from Francine in Waynesboro within minutes. Waynesboro meant five more miles but our legs felt good and three miles were downhill. Waynesboro has a population of around 21,000 and you won't believe it but spandex was invented here. We also met Tom, a 65-year-old Texan who is on his FIFTH!!! time cycling around the USA (10,000 miles each trip).

Francine invited us to her house and after a spoiled evening yesterday we just got another one. Francine fed us delicious fish with veggies which was accompanied by our little wine present.

At the end we finished with fresh made gingerbread and lemon sauce so that we should definitely be loaded up on carbs for tomorrow's trip to Lexington, VA. Life is good and full of gingerbread.

Day 5 – Barking Dogs won't Bite

That's at least a German saying and the only thing I could think of when we got surrounded by four little flea bags which even tried to attack and eventually got support from a fifth one. We discussed this topic with Ross, one of our Warm Showers hosts, and he recommended to jump of the bike and yell at them. It worked, they wouldn't give up immediately but were definitely confused and took off after a little bit. Good for them that they didn't have to experience the little can of spicy spray I am carrying with me.

The day was beautiful and we started in Waynesboro where we spent a nice night at Francine's house and due to our little detour yesterday, we didn't have to go back into the hilly mountains but instead could cycle through the valley. Vesuvius was supposed to be halfway of today's trip and before that we even stopped at Rhema Lake for a quick coffee. This little detour was also the reason we ran into the dogs later. As soon as we got back onto Cold Springs Rd it was an easy ride to Vesuvius where we had to get lunch at Gertie's Country Store. Man, people are so friendly here, 50% of all cars driving on the opposite side of the road wave to us and there was still more friendliness to come. Rebecca, another Warm Showers host, left us a voicemail that we could stay at their house tonight. But it's not just a house, it's a huge farmhouse surrounded by 25 acres of land. Once we arrived, we received so much friendliness and hospitality that it's hard to find words for it.

Rebecca and her husband made quiche, salad and cookies for us and we even played a new game called Rumis after dinner (Rebecca and I won :-P) Now we are definitely ready for bed and geared up for the next stage tomorrow. Today we clocked in 50 miles and made it after

Lexington, VA. We don't have a clear target for tomorrow but probably between 50-65 miles to Daleville or even farther.

Y'all have a good night and a good start to your morning.

Day 6 – 300 Miles and still in Virginia

And this won't change for the next days. Virginia is not such a big state but the route we are taking doesn't go the direct way so it will be at least four more days until we will reach Kentucky.

It was hard to leave the Grey Fox Farm where we stayed yesterday. Rebecca and Lee were such a wonderful couple and sent us off on our 50 mile ride to Daleville, VA with a great breakfast. We will always keep you in our mind and hope that our ways cross each other again in the future.

The route was pretty calm and not many cars or dogs crossed our way. But we finally met another TransAm cyclist. Ken, who started in San Diego, went along the Southern Tier and looked as tanned as Tanning Mom (google her if you don't remember her) but assured us, that he only had 18 sunny days out of his 60 and 42 were actually rainy. He is cycling 10,000 miles for cancer and will go all the way up to Rhode Island and then back on the Northern Tier (Facebook: Kens 10,000 miles for childhood cancer)

We arrived in Buchanan around lunch time and I was so excited to find a German restaurant on Google Maps. Unfortunately selling German food to Virginians must be as difficult as selling a Toyota Prius to them because it was out of business. *

We found the Good Times Cafe at the other end of the city and I don't want to know what's going on there on Friday (see pic below) but they served us a terrific burger and we had a great chat with the owner whose first job was to put mail sacks on poles along the railroad tracks so the trains could pick them up with long hooks while they drove by at 50mph.

Eventually we arrived in Daleville where the Appalachian

14

Trail crosses the Transamerica bicycle trail. We ran into a lot of hikers, chatted with some of them and wished them good luck.
Tomorrow, we will start early to avoid the heat and get some extra miles on the road.

*To be honest, I love Pickup Country

Day 7 – ONE Week of Cycling

…and it has been terrific. 6 ½ days of sunshine and almost 400 miles into the country, our experiences reach from meeting fellow Transamers to staying at people's places and enjoying their Southern hospitality.

Today's route took us up to Catawba, followed by Christiansburg, Radford and finally Dublin. Since it got pretty hot the last days, we started off at 7am and cycled three hours without break until we finally spotted a nice rest area close to a church. The miles before were characterized by A LOT of "No Trespassing" signs, so we didn't want to risk our first angry encounter with a Virginian who complains that we leaned our bikes against his valuable fence or barbed wire. Around lunch time we arrived in Christiansburg on top of a steep mountain and Subway had to make us huge sandwiches to load up on fuel for the afternoon. It was a good decision to start early and it felt great to have cycled 47 miles until lunch. Unlike the days before we could take it a little slower in the afternoon and we had to since the sun was burning and there were still a lot of climbs ahead of us. We decided to camp at Claytor Lake State Park but I haven't seen a much more confusing system than the one at this park/campground. Due to the absence of a ranger, there was an honor system for the fee in place but not only we wouldn't understand how it worked, it was also 30!!! bucks for a tent site. Long story short, another member of the Patel clan got a little richer tonight and we are again having a bed, free Wi-Fi, TV, …. (60% of mid-sized motels and hotel properties all over the US are owned by people of Indian origin, mainly with the last name Patel)

Total mileage today was 72 but it seems like we have the tough long rolling mountains behind us. Tomorrow's route will take us through cities like Newbern, Draper, Mad Meadows, Wytheville, Rural Retreat, ... I doubt that any of those will serve us Starbucks coffee.

Highlight of the day: Finished our first Transamerica Map.

Good deed of the day: Carrying Mr. Turtle, who decided to take a sunbath on the road, to the other side of the street.

Day 8 – The Smell of Roadkill

 .... surprised and shocked us today a lot of times. Sometimes we could already smell a dead animal before we would see it. Possums are definitely the unlucky ones in Virginia trying to cross the roads. We didn't even know that there are vultures in Virginia, too. They just seem to wait until a squirrel, possum, cat or rabbit unsuccessfully crosses the road.

Today's route took us from Dublin, VA via Wytheville and Atkins to Marion. It was a 60-mile ride and we decided not to follow the map. It was a wise decision since we probably saved 30 hilly miles back into the Appalachians. On our way we took it slow and stopped at Carter Wayside Park for a coffee break and at Skeeters in Wytheville for a Slaw Dog and BLT. Wytheville is located in Wythe County, named after George Wythe, who signed the Declaration of Independence. In addition to that, Edith Bolling Wilson, second wife and First Lady of Woodrow Wilson was born here.

So, enough history. Let's talk about the future. There will be Hayters. No, I am not talking about the new adidas campaign but about a 1,500 ft. elevation climb we have to master tomorrow at Hayters Gap. Even our excellent Google Maps skills, which maneuvered us easily through the Appalachians, couldn't find us a sneaky way around this monster. So don't be surprised if we are in a bad mood tomorrow or not able to post about Day 9.

But today, life is good!

Day 9 – But I would cycle 500 miles

......and I would cycle 500 more just to be the man who cycled a thousand miles to fall down at your door
Well said Proclaimers, well said and we are proud to announce that we hit 500 miles today. Wahoo. But what a fight it was. As predicted yesterday, Hayters Gap wouldn't be an easy hill to cycle up. 4 ½ miles straight up to 3,000ft. We stopped a few times but we conquered it within an hour. However, we felt like Tour de France cyclists who make it up the Alp D'Huez. Ready to load up on carbs, we couldn't find anything better than a gas station in Rosedale where we at least got some pizza slices. It was only fifteen more miles to Council but Google Maps showed 2 ½ hours and was damn right because we underestimated another climb up to 2,800ft (seriously we feel like we are cycling in the Swiss Alps). Unfortunately, Ashlin's knee started to twinge a little bit and since we are in one of the states with the greatest hospitality, we stopped at a nice house and asked if we could set-up our tent in their yard. They immediately offered us a bedroom but we didn't want to cause too much inconvenience and ended up being driven to our final spot of the day only a few miles away. It's the William P. Harris Recreation Park where we set up our camp in a tiny house which is on a playground for kids. So, we will sleep surrounded by drawings of Spongebob, Mickey Mouse and Winnie Pooh. Wayne, another TransAm cyclist picked a sleeping spot on a stage nearby and we chatted a little bit. He is from Williamsburg, VA where he also started last week. He is planning 50-60 mile rides so we might see him from now on more often.
The park and surrounding don't offer much food or groceries but we still had a 3-course dinner starting with Breakfast Skillet, Chili Mac and Hot Apple Cobbler for

dessert. Thanks Mountain House for offering such a great variety of freeze dried food. Hope the raccoons (for my German friends, I would translate them Wash-Bears) will be quiet later while going through our stuff.

PS: Special thanks to Chilhowie Coffee Shop and their owner and daughter who made us a great Iced Coffee for free this morning.

Day 10 – Virginia is Simply too Beautiful

…and that's why we decided to stay a day longer. We started pretty early from Council where we had our first real outdoor night. It got a little cold in the morning and we woke up a few times during the night to weird noises outside but we felt rested when we got up.

Our route today took us through Birchleaf, Haysi and Sandlick. Ashlin's knee felt a little better but we still took it pretty slowly up the three hills after Haysi and before the Breaks Interstate Park. The park is situated at the border of Virginia and Kentucky and we were already excited to cross our first state boarder by bike but once we got up to the top, the view made us thinking and we decided to stay in Virginia one more night. Even as it meant we would have only cycled 30 miles, we always said that we would take some days off in between to rest, relax or to go sightseeing. Our alternative would have been a church or stealth camping without all the amenities we got here. We were able to do laundry, eat in and make a fire. Definitely worth it.

Tomorrow's route will bring us then to Kentucky on a 60+ mile ride so we better get some rest in our tent now.

Y'all have a good night and stay tuned for our first pictures and lines from Kentucky.

Life is good.

Day 11 – Kentucky, Dogs and Google Maps

Oh what a day. It started early and a little slow but it got more interesting every minute.

We left the Breaks Interstate campground around 7am since the forecast showed temperatures in the 80s and we had a 65+ mile ride ahead of us. The park is pretty close to the state line. It only took us 20-30 minutes to make it to Kentucky and to be honest, it was a great feeling to cross one state by bike and ride into another. After being only a few minutes in Kentucky we were looking for a good spot for breakfast and a sign promised us a bakery at a local Bed and Breakfast in Elkhorn City. The owner was super nice and must have tried to compete against the friendliness we received in Virginia. She was so happy to see TransAm cyclists at her bakery that she wouldn't let us go without taking a picture of us eating a New York Cheesecake and Cappuccino Cupcake for breakfast.

Once back on the road we had to make a big decision. Google Maps showed a one-hour faster route than the TransAm maps and sometime you need nuts and sometimes you need balls uhh bolts, so I made the decision to trust Google again since it hadn't disappointed us so far. We cycled all along the beautiful Elkhorn Creek and refueled in Jenkins, KY before continuing on our own route.

Many Transamers warn that you will encounter a lot of chasing dogs in Kentucky and they were right. Luckily the first two which tried to catch us must have been on an unhealthy diet because we didn't even have to cycle hard to outrun them but a little later that day we had three flea bags directly ahead of us. We stopped cycling and I had the pepper spray ready but fortunately the owner called them and they retreated. Three others tried to chase us later that day but vs two downhill cyclists they didn't stand a chance.

Coming back to Google Maps. Well, well, well. We were definitely faster today than the other way but I don't know what Google thought when it directed us to a 2.8-mile section of gravel road. It was pretty tough and we had to push our bikes for a mile or so but luckily we made it and arrived in Hindman, KY around 4PM. Hindman has a special hostel place for cyclists but due to the strong winter they are still repairing their facilities. We ended up at the local church and ran into Wayne and Rick, who we met three days ago in Council the first time, and Ryan who is also cycling the TransAm. We all got dinner at the Pizza place across the street, chatted, laughed and had a good time. All without alcohol because believe it or not we are in a Dry County. All five of us are sleeping in the facilities of the Youth Ministry and it will be interesting to see who snores the most. I am already looking forward to grabbing a beer with Ryan in two days when we should arrive in Berea, KY.

Life is good and even chasing dogs can't change that.

Y'all enjoy yourselves now.

Day 12 – We are in the Blasting Zone

 At least we cycled through two and we were even supposed to turn off our phones but we didn't and nothing exploded. It was probably related to the coal mining industry which is huge in Kentucky but the opinions couldn't differ more. We talked to a couple of people and we understand that there are a lot of pros and cons. After we left Hindman this morning we stopped in Hazard which boomed during its good coal days but since 90% of its coal reserves are gone, many people live off of food stamps and many even turn to drugs. A fruit stand retailer took a lot of his time to talk with us and we enjoyed chatting with him. He even offered us his farmhouse to camp at but it was too far. At least we could accept a free apple and a piece of cantaloupe with salt!!! Yes, we were also skeptical but it tasted good and he even puts salt on watermelon. Try it out.

Our route after Hazard had a lot of hills and dogs but we were able to manage them pretty well. We rode together with Ryan and we kept pushing each other so that we ended up in Buckhorn, our destination for tonight, around 1pm. Since there was only a campsite, no restaurants and it's in a dry county we decided to push another 18 miles and ended up in Booneville which is supposed to be in a dry county too but they are selling beer at the market BUT not on Sundays and guess what day it is. It seems like we need to move on to get our first beer as a reward for more than 700 miles of cycling so far.

Tomorrow's route will take us to Berea but the hills just don't want to stop. It's always a fight up the hills with more than 40lbs of gear and we are actually one of the Light-Travelers. I wouldn't be surprised if all the shooting holes in the signs, which show uphill switchbacks, come from angry cyclists who just don't want to go uphill anymore.

Well, we don't want to complain, life is good, we are with new friends and there will be another beautiful day tomorrow.

Last but not least, I want to thank our moms for their support and let them know that we are doing well. Thanks for making us who we are.

Happy Mother's Day

Day 13 – Martin in the Eye of the Storm

After a relaxing night under a pavilion behind a church with three other TransAm companions, we left early to avoid the heat and make it to Berea, KY before thunderstorms or heat would make cycling a pain. The hilly part definitely seems to be over and today's little humps didn't scare us anymore. Our legs felt good, so it was not a surprise that we already arrived in Berea around lunch time. Again, we went with Ryan who reached out to a nice woman on Warm Showers, Maya, who was willing to host us three at her place. Maya also directed us to the Welcome Center where super friendly people gave us an overview about the city. After a little chat we decided to grab lunch and found a very nice Amish deli close to the city center.

Since Maya wouldn't be home before 5 pm, we used the time to relax and find a nice café to sit outside in the sun. Unfortunately, the super humid air, which accompanied us throughout the day, built monster clouds much faster than expected and once we got to a very nice looking café sirens went off indicating approaching severe thunderstorms. It definitely scared us a little since we are not so familiar with the weather here and you keep seeing tornado shelters every now and then. We decided to head to Maya's place and made it there safely. The weather didn't look too bad so I took off my panniers and headed to the market to get some dinner for Maya and us three. On my way down I had to pass one intersection and the traffic lights were swinging like in the typical hurricane and storm news on TV but the sky still didn't look too bad. When I left the market I could hear thunder but 0.7 miles to Maya's place seemed to be manageable. It was not. It took maybe 1-2 minutes and hail came down, followed by monsoon like rain. Luckily, I found some shelter in a small flower shop where I waited until the worst was over. It definitely showed us how different the weather is down here and how fast it can change. We will keep that in mind for our next days. The evening went great. We all cooked together, baked banana bread, chatted and just had a good time.

Berea means also that we are done with our second set of maps. Wahoo.

Life is good, even in the eye of a thunderstorm.

Day 14 – Becoming a Kentucky Farmer

That was at least my wish after we spoke to Charlie this morning. We were riding our bikes from Berea, where we had a delicious breakfast with Maya, to Harrodsburg. Two hours into our trip we saw a farmer on his tractor. He shouted and we shouted but we finally decided to turn around and chat with him. Charlie quit his job one year ago and is now working on his family's farm. He noticed that there were a lot of cyclists passing by his property until he realized that the land is located directly along the Transamerica Trail. He wants to start a bed and breakfast or hostel for cyclists and we tried to answer all the questions he had. We learned that people from Kentucky are super friendly, so I just asked him if we could sit on his tractor. Moments later we all had the chance to sit on his machine and take some pictures with him. Man, he was the nicest person we met today and one of the nicest we met during our whole trip. It's definitely worth to start a conversation with anybody along this trip. Even at lunch we invited Forrest, a local guy, to our table and tried to answer all his questions about Germany and our trip. Funny fact: He was a runner during high school. I guess he had to hear: "Run Forrest, run" a lot

The cycling part went slowly since a very strong headwind blew in our face the whole day. I guess the first two weeks can be considered as the perfect training for the rest of the trip. Be it hill climbing by bike or surviving 20mph headwinds, we should be ready for the next six weeks. It has been fourteen days and we cycled almost 800 miles and a total of 77 hours.

Now we have to digest our good country cookin' dinner. We tried Hot Brown which is sliced ham and turkey, covered with cheese gravy and topped with bacon and

tomatoes baked golden brown.

Life is good, especially when you can sit on a tractor. Thanks Charlie!

Day 15 – Beer, Saloons and Whiskey

168 miles – check.

New Haven, KY – check

Exhausted but happy – check

We started early in Harrodsburg and were on the road around 7:30AM. Three hours later we already had more than 30 miles on the cycling computer. We also got a call from Ryan, our fellow traveler from the last days who went 25 miles longer yesterday and wanted to see where we were. He was already in Bardstown which was our destination for our lunch break and we decided to meet up for lunch and cycle the remaining 20 miles to New Haven together. On our way we even visited one of the local whiskey distilleries which looked more like a prison.

Our final stop, New Haven, is a little off the route but famous for its railway museum and also the only spot where you can find some lodging for miles. The Sherwood Inn is a 100-year-old building and it definitely has a lot of charm and character. The saloon downstairs served us beer and burgers and we talked to some local guys telling us stories about the prohibition and Jesse James. You never know how much truth is in these stories but they are always fun to listen to.

Tomorrow we will head to Mammoth Cave for some sightseeing and a day off. Kentucky remains a very great and friendly state.

Day 16 – Becoming a Mammoth

 Or at least a camper at the Mammoth Cave Campground in Kentucky. The caves are not situated along the route but Adventure Cycling put an additional detour of this loop on their maps and we decided to take the chance and visit the cave tomorrow. That means that tomorrow will be a day off or at least half a day off. Let's see how we feel after climbing up and down 400 steps and walking two miles in a cave.

Today has been great and we met with a lot of interesting people. We had to say goodbye for now to Ryan who didn't go on the 80-mile Mammoth Cave loop and who is heading directly to Murphysboro. Good Luck Buddy. Shortly after we arrived at the campground we met Nathan, a 28-year-old Australian who traveled seven months through South America and who is now motorcycling through the US on his 700lbs Kawasaki. He has his campsite next to us so we enjoyed his company at our campfire. Somehow we were even able to make one of the biggest campfires with awful wet wood and got even more guests. Bob and Janeene, both retired and driving around in of the biggest RVs we have ever seen, talked to us for a while and showed us the interior of their nice ride. It's clearly hard to go back to a 2-person tent once you see a queen sized bed in a RV BUT we like our tent and will enjoy a great night outdoors.

Highlight of today's 70-mile ride was crossing into Central Time, which felt like a huge milestone. Somehow we will go back to Eastern tomorrow. 'Merica, you confuse me

Btw, talking about milestones. We visited Kentucky Stonehenge today.

Y'all have an awesome night.

Day 17 – "Day Off"

Which meant that we only cycled 42 miles instead of our usual 60+. The day started great after we slept in at the Mammoth Cave Campground. Our 2-hour cave tour was scheduled for 9AM and since we made it to Central time the night felt really long and relaxing.

The cave was absolutely worth the additional 80 miles of cycling. It's the longest cave system known in the world and includes some cool parts like Fat Man's Misery which is a very narrow part of the cave. We also learned from another visitor that you can do 3 or 6-hour crawling tours with headlamps. Well, we still wanted to get some pedaling done and chose the 2-mile walking tour. Once we came out, the sun was grilling us but we still decided to cycle to Sonora. It was hot, it was humid and it was hilly but we made it. In the end it was not quite the easy day we were hoping for.

We found a bed and breakfast place mentioned on our maps and we contacted the owner, Charles Thurman, who was happy to accommodate us. Charlie was in the oil business and worked for a long time in New Orleans but came back and restored his family's house, where we are staying, and two other places in Sonora. The main house is over 100 years old and filled with a lot of history and memories. He gave us the tour and it was impressive to see all the old memorabilia like his grandfather's camera which shot a picture of the house 100 years ago.

We are now sitting in the house's sunroom and recapping our last 17 days. It has been an awesome adventure so far and we should hit 1,000 miles tomorrow.

Y'all enjoy yourselves now.

Day 18 – We are Singing in the Rain

 After 17 rain-free days our lucky streak was over and a lot of rain joined us on our trip to Rough River Dam State Resort Park. It poured so heavily that we interrupted our trip around lunch time and waited under a pavilion behind a church for an hour for the rain to stop. We changed into dry clothes and laid out our wet ones, followed by brewing a coffee and tea. Unfortunately, the surrounding fields must have been harvested days before because moments later I had a sneeze attack which didn't stop until we left. When the bicycle computer read 52 miles we arrived at our motel for the night. We are not the only adventurers here. A few fishermen participating in a bass fishing tournament are staying here too and we chatted for a little bit and had a beer together. Their tournament was almost as enjoyable as our rain ride since most of them didn't catch anything. We think the worst should be over and hope that both the fishermen and us will have a successful day tomorrow.

Last but not least, one big highlight was hitting the 1,000-mile mark during today's ride. Only 2,600 miles left.

Day 19 – Eye to Eye with a Snake

Yes, after weeks of only seeing dead animals on the road (most of them super flat and/or super stinky) we saw our first 5-6 foot snake halfway on the road. We have been nice to all kind of animals; we rescued a lot of turtles from the roads and snuggled with donkeys, horses and goats. Today it was time to get eye to eye with this hissing reptile so I grabbed the longest stick I could find (probably not longer than 1 ½ foot) and tried to get it off the road. There are no venomous snakes in Kentucky except for Copperheads and some rattlers but this one didn't look or sounded like any of them. Also, its round eyes seemed to be a good indicator for a non-venomous cow/chicken snake. BUT you never know from which terrarium this deadly slithering creature escaped from so I was super careful and once I got my stick close to it, it decided to move its head up and wait. Eventually it retreated after I made a lot of vibrations on the road.

Back to cycling: The morning started with an awesome breakfast at the Dam General Store in Falls of Rough. We met Anthony, who works there, the night before when they made us a mouth-watering burger and we decided that we had to come back for breakfast. We got what we expected: A delicious omelet, pancakes and a bacon egg cheese biscuit. Thanks Anthony and sorry that we didn't catch each other this morning.

After breakfast, we started our 69-mile journey to Sebree, KY and not even ten miles into our day we met two guys who started their west-east journey a month ago in San Diego and who are riding supported by the Bike the US for MS team. Almost there guys. Keep pedaling. The empty roads took us to Utica where we decided to stop for lunch. A 500 people city with nothing more than a gas station. An older guy saw our bikes and started talking to us. He was friendly but seemed poor or even homeless, indicated by the fact that one of the local ladies gave him a mango. He grew up in San Diego and kept repeating the sentence "I should have settled down" and it was kind of sad to talk to him. I took him with me into the gas station and asked if I could buy him lunch but not more than a corn dog was his wish.

We kept cycling and dark clouds and a strong head and side wind followed us along the trip. Well, seems like the clouds weren't very thick cause we got sunburnt, but we ended up at an awesome place to cure our sore legs and sunburns. The First Baptist Church holds its doors open for cyclists and we are enjoying the comfort of couches, laundry, snacks and hot showers.

Dinner was at a local diner and I want to thank Ashlin for inviting me. Also for surprising me this morning with a candlelit muffin. Yes, it's my birthday and I am thankful for all the birthday wishes I received today. Even though I couldn't be with most of you guys today, I definitely thought of you.

Y'all are great people!

Day 20 – A River Runs Through it

 This is the name of one of our favorite movies and today it was time to cross a big river. The Ohio River defines the boarder between Kentucky and Illinois and you might already know what I am going to say. Yes, we made it to Illinois. This is our third state on this journey but we won't spend so much time here before going straight to Missouri.

The day started pretty normal. We had a great night at the First Baptist Church in Sebree and they really know their stuff. They host around 250 cyclists a year and are prepared for everything. It was great to stay there and their offer of staying longer than one night was even more tempting this morning when we saw the big rain clouds in the sky. We were hoping that the rain might stop after a nice breakfast at the local diner and we were right. It still rained a little bit on us but the "nice" headwind dried us pretty quickly. Our lunch spot after 45 miles was in Marion and only a few moments after we sat down Wayne saw us in the cafe and came in to chat. We met him in Council, VA and stayed at two or three places with him together. Marion was already his final destination of the day so we said goodbye and took off to cycle another 20 miles. The highlight was clearly the ferry which took us from Kentucky to Cave in Rock. I was a little sad to leave Kentucky. It has been a great state and you never know what lies ahead of you. Even the dogs became very friendly today. One little pooch didn't want to leave our side and followed us for half a mile until I decided to cycle back with him to his home.

Tonight we are staying in Elizabethtown, IL where we also had our first fried catfish. Apparently this is some kind of local dish and caught in the Ohio River which flows directly in front of us. It was very delicious but I guess after 67 miles mostly everything fried will taste very yummy. Tomorrow we will head to Carbondale which is one of the bigger cities along the way. We will also try to get our bikes checked at the local bike shop. Life is good and y'all have a good night.

Day 21 – A Short Tale from Carbondale

 We finally made it to a city with a population bigger than 1,000. Carbondale, home of Southern Illinois University, was our final stop after 67 miles through the "Land of Lincoln". A college town also meant that we would have the chance to get a good coffee and different food than what the gas stations offer along the way. It has been 1,222 miles since we left the east coast and it also means that we are ~1/3 done with our trip, or 2/3 not done ☺ A perfect timing to let the bikes get a general checkup at the local bike store. We hope that Katy and Perry, or Smokey and Bandit or Hans and Franz (we haven't given them names yet) will be fine and ready to ride with us another 2,400 miles. Once we dropped them off we found a nearby cafe which provided us with Cuban Espresso and an Iced Latte. Finally! It was a perfect spot to relax and very soon our Warm Showers host for tonight showed up. Jack is a 68-year-old retiree who was willing to host us for tonight. He made us delicious breaded chicken breasts and even baked a cake. We are getting so spoiled during this trip and we loved sharing our stories with him. He took over the gas station business of his parents, founded a fire extinguisher business, sold insurances, built wooden pallets and owned an ice cream shop. You can probably imagine that he had a lot of stories to tell.

Tomorrow's trip will take us to Chester, IL which also marks the last stop in Illinois before we will cross the mighty Mississippi and enter into Missouri.

Life is good and even better when you had a Cuban Espresso.

Day 22 – One Mississippi, two Mississippis...

... and 36 Mississippi uhh miles until we saw the mighty Mississippi River but we are still in Illinois and haven't crossed over to Missouri yet.

We started late in Carbondale this morning since we had to wait until the bike shop opened. We used the free time to invite our Warm Showers host Jack for breakfast and continued our dialogue from the night before. Fortunately, there were no major hiccups with our bikes so we picked them up shortly after 10am and put our panniers back on. Only moments after we left Jack's house, it started pouring and the rain followed us until we decided to take a lunch break in Neunert at Bottoms Up Family Bar and Grill. Kristi was a wonderful waitress and the cook made us a delicious lunch. We were completely soaked and enjoyed being inside waiting until the rain stopped. Eventually we wanted to leave the restaurant but a man didn't want us to and even persisted to pay our check. It was such a generous gesture and we enjoyed talking to him. His name was Juan Sanchez (I hope I got that right) and he worked for the US Army, partly in Germany which was a country he loved. We shared stories and chatted until the rain finally stopped. It's always hard to leave those kind of people, and the same is true for our Warm Showers hosts, but we still had 23 miles left and didn't want to arrive in Chester, IL too late. Chester is hometown of Popeye the sailorman and the route to this famous town was a mix of middle of nowhere and a busy coal truck road but fortunately the trucks were mainly on the other side of the road. Our idea was to reward ourselves with a stay at a hotel but who would have known that a motel in a city with 800 people also gets sold out sometimes during the year.

Luckily the Chester Eagles Fraternity offers a shed with

nine bunk beds to cyclists and also a warm shower so we were happy to find this place for the night.

Tomorrow we will cross the Mississippi and enter our fourth state Missouri but before that we want to check out the Popeye museum.

Life is good, even if you sleep in a bunk bed.

Day 23 – A Night in Jail

Yes, we ended up in a jail tonight but let's start with the cycling part. The day was pretty cool and not only because of temperatures in the 40s this morning and not higher than 60 during the day. We started late in Chester, IL where we wanted to check out the Popeye "Museum". They definitely had everything you can imagine when you think of Popeye and we got some little patches. We are trying to get a little something in each state we are cycling and the patches seemed like the perfect lightweight memory. Only a few miles later we were ready to cross the Mighty Mississippi but not without a quick stop at the bronze statue of Popeye shortly before the bridge. A huge mining truck stopped and I talked to the driver for a bit. He was calling the police to let them stop the traffic from the other side of the bridge, otherwise he wouldn't fit. This was our chance to get an empty road to cycle over the river and we took off the police car following us. It kind of felt like an escort and we really liked it. It was also our last highlight in Illinois because we entered into Missouri on the other side of the river. Our fourth state started super flat. Unfortunately, not very long and we returned to our up and down pattern of rolling hills. Some pretty tough ones but after 34 miles the Crown Valley Brewery offered a perfect break. The pulled bison sandwich and the BBQ bison pizza gave us enough power for the remaining fourteen miles to Farmington. After 48 miles to Farmington we found our place for tonight at Al's Place Bike Hostel in Farmington which was a jail in the past. There was even a famous jailbreak in 1932 when people from outside tried to free the 31 prisoners with nine dynamite sticks. Only seven were able to escape, the rest were stunned by the huge explosion and out of the seven, two were killed while running and five were recaptured. The explosion was heard three miles away and the 14-pound steel window was found two blocks away on top of the local high school.

Nowadays the jail serves cyclists as a hostel with a lot of great amenities like washer and dryer, showers, TV, kitchen, Wi-Fi and a lot of memorabilia. Since we are the only ones here, it's all ours tonight.

Not much else to say about Farmington except that we found a German supermarket Aldi which made me very happy ☺

Now we are ready for our comfy beds to get some rest for a 60-mile day tomorrow.

Day 24 – Support from Katy Perry

 Helene Fischer, The Offspring and many other music artists. We knew it would be a hilly day and we decided to try out some musical distraction. We connected a phone with our mini loudspeaker and we were all set for a 60-mile tour to Ellington Missouri. The music pushed us so much that we hit 30 miles after only 2 ½ hours. We were flying through the country and this actually reminds me of the movie American Flyers, great cycling movie and probably one of Kevin Costner's few good ones. Sorry, honest opinion. First break was at Pilot Knob. The Battle of Pilot Knob in the fall of 1864 was a notable clash in the area during the Civil War and the city still maintains a museum. We ran into two other cyclists, a couple who was going on their 35-mile morning ride. They were super friendly and the husband even sang the Flipper song in German for us. The positive vibe didn't disappear because moments later an employee of Reeds Bakery in Pilot Knob handed us two donuts for free which we loved. Probably one of the best donuts we ever had and we would stick to this opinion even if we had paid for them.

The rest of the trip went along a lot of rolling hills but we kept the fast momentum and arrived in Ellington before 3pm. This gives us enough time to relax for tomorrow's 69 Miler which will bring us to Houston in Texas County but still Missouri.

Day 25 – Houston, We Have

......defeated the Ozarks and arrived in Missouri's counterpart of Texas' city with the same name. It's hard to believe but we cycled 72 miles, climbed more than 4,000 ft. and everything in less than 6 ½ hours but man these hills from Ellington to Summersville really tried to scare the heck out of us. We managed it well and we are proud that we didn't even have to get off our bikes and push them once. Slowly but steadily we cycled up the dozen really steep hills, always in mind the upcoming reward of speeding downhill. We started early at 730AM and the weather and traffic were in our favor so we were more or less done with the hilly part at our lunch break.

We received some questions of how many calories we are burning and how fast we can go through hilly parts. I decided to track one hour of cycling today with the App Strava. It was impressive to see that we climbed 1,200ft and burned more than 600 calories in one hour while maintaining 9.7mph. Other highlights on our route today were a bald eagle which circled above us and presented itself in a tree next to the road (see pic), checking out a fire tower and adding more animals to our roadkill list: a beaver, which was the size of a huge pillow, and a few armadillos.

Now we really feel every mile in our muscles and hope that tomorrow's 60 miler will loosen up our sore bodies.

Day 26 – Staying Dry

Yeah, this was our priority for today. The day always starts with a check of the weather app to get a feeling for the right clothing (poor society, what happened to just going to look outside and check the weather). The forecast showed a lot of rain and the radar also promised a lot of rainy clouds moving to our location. Once we got started, we had the sun behind and the dark clouds ahead of us and not even thirty minutes into our cycling day the first downpour came down on us. Fortunately, we found shelter under a tree next to some cows and the rain didn't last very long. Our first break was in Hartville where we found a good diner to load up on calories and to chat with the locals. It's hard to answer the same questions of "Where are you from?" "Where are you cycling?" with the same friendliness but we did well.

It was only 25 miles to our final target Marshfield but we could see the darks clouds constricting the circle of good weather in which me moved. The wind picked up and we decided to find some shelter in an abandoned house along the road. Seconds after we went in, the downpour started and lasted at least 20-30 minutes. We liked our little haunted house and took the chance to enjoy our apple pie snacks and some coffee. The remaining 17 miles were characterized by no villages, stores and not even any houses. I guess pretty similar to what will expect us once we cycle through Kansas. Minutes before another big downpour started we were already in our motel for tonight. I guess we can call it the day of good timing.

Day 27 – Finishing with a Jackhammer

 It was a short cycling day but the less cycling was overcompensated by an extra amount of hospitality. We cycled from Marshfield, MO all along Historic Route 66 to Springfield, MO which was only a 25 mile ride but the plan was to meet up with members of Ashlin's family and get two shorter days instead of one long one to relax a little bit. Donald and Laura welcomed us in their incredibly beautiful house and the moment we put our bikes aside we immediately felt at home. Maybe also because their kids drew us a "Welcome Ashlin and Martin" sign. We had such a great time playing games, chatting and enjoying a delicious dinner at the fire outside that it simply couldn't get better, but it did.

They decided to take us and their kids Elle and Kaya to Andy's Frozen Custard which looked like a 50s diner, fully illuminated and THE place to go for desserts. Apparently they have franchises all over the country but we have never seen them before. The menu looked like we could load up on the burned calories very easily and Ashlin and I ended up with a James Brownie Funky Jackhammer which is a vanilla frozen custard blended with creamy peanut butter and brownies, then filled with hot fudge. Nothing more to say ☺

Day 28 – You Will Probab Lee Love This

 Well, another wonderful day comes to an end and it started already wonderful. It must have been the delicious breakfast which Laura prepared for us this morning. Pancakes, bacon, eggs and coffee help everyone start the day with a smile. Oh and of course drinking a glass of raw milk which was sooo yummy. It was also pretty hard to leave Donald's and Laura's beautiful place but we had 35 miles of cycling ahead of us and Donald even made sure that we would add another six miles within Springfield to get the (I quote) "most beautiful scenic awesome safe bike route to Everton, MO" which included the Route 66 visitor center, the town square and the McDaniel Park where we took a picture for Ashlin's uncle Lee! It's at least something we can do to say thank you to one/some of our readers and we are going to try to find more of these special things for our friends and family. "Unfortunately" the circle of our supporters is growing everyday and today's highlight was that Ashlin's former babysitter, who now lives "only 1 ½ hour" away from our final stop, decided to meet us for dinner. She picked us up and believe it or not we ended up driving back to Springfield where we started this morning. And just so we could eat at THE Bass Pro Shops which is actually where Bass Pro Shops was founded and has one of their biggest stores. It's an awesome place with ponds full of trout, stuffed bears and elks and even live alligators. We enjoyed the dinner buffet at their restaurant and I am pretty sure they didn't make a lot of money by feeding two hungry TransAm cyclists who didn't have lunch today. So, all should be good for tomorrow's trip which will take us to Kansas – our fifth state. Wahoo.
Life is good and I will probably Miss-ouri.

Day 29 – The Best Trips end with Ribs

...... especially when it's endless ribfest at Ribs Crib BBQ which was our spot for tonight's dinner. As yesterday we can only underline that it's a bad idea to offer all you can eat to TransAm cyclists ☺

Today has been a great day. The weather during the night didn't look and sound very promising since a lot of thunderstorms hit our area but the sun was back once we left Everton, MO. We could still see thunderstorm clouds in the south but they never got close to us so that our day turned into a hot and humid cycling day. Unfortunately, gas stations, restaurants and grocery stores are getting scarcer and we had to cycle 30 miles to Golden City until we got our "breakfast" which was actually a lunch since they stopped serving breakfast 30 minutes before we arrived. Cooky's Cafe seemed to be a popular spot among cyclists and they even had a cyclist guest book where we found the names of two fellow TransAmers who we were cycling with a few days ago. Christian Bale Batman Voice: "So, if you can read this Wayne and Ryan, we are coming for you and the chase has begun ☺"

From Golden City it was only another 30 miles until our final destination Pittsburg, KS and the fact that we would cross into Kansas in less than two hours of cycling kept us pedaling with >15mph average – maybe also due to a favorable tailwind. It was not even 3pm when we arrived in Pittsburg where we noticed a lot of Gorilla statues – the mascot of Pittsburg State University. We didn't want to go to Gorilla Village which is their big pre-game area but instead it was time to take the opportunity to enjoy a delicious coffee at the Seattle-based coffee shop with the green mermaid in their logo. We don't want to advertise too much ☺ A 65-mile day comes to an end and y'all enjoy yourselves now.

Day 30 – Water, Water and more Water

Yes, we got a lot of it today. We started into the day pretty dry but the dark clouds were only a few miles away. We pushed hard and arrived in Girard after an hour. Girard apparently has one of the biggest US flags but it can't be so big because we didn't notice it. Since the clouds got darker we thought it would be better to take an early breakfast break and to wait a little bit to let the rainy clouds move over. They more or less disappeared and we left knowing from our radar checking that we would face rain eventually. It only took 30 minutes until a light rain started and accompanied us until Walnut where it got stronger and we decided to take another break. It was also the only spot on our route which offered food before our final stop. The lunch break turned into a Spanish or Mexican siesta since this strong downpour lasted for almost two hours which we spent inside the gas station. I guess if we had waited another two hours we would have had to help out and work there but we decided to leave. It's definitely tough to start cycling again after resting for a while but we found our rhythm and cycled through the rain which stopped half an hour before Chanute, KS – our final stop. The sun was back, it got hot and we were missing the water so much that we decided to jump into the pool.

Can't get wetter uhh better than this.

Day 31 – Quick Stop at the ER

There is nothing more important than refreshing your tetanus shots on a TransAm cycling trip. However, the circumstances could have been better. We left this morning knowing that the rain would accompany us for a big portion of the day but the day shouldn't last very long. The endless rain showers have really left their marks everywhere and are definitely causing some trouble for cyclists, be it the dirt which collects around the chain or the slippery conditions of the roads. We weren't even four miles into our trip when an old railroad crossing caused Ashlin's bicycle slip to the side. She fell on her right side and we immediately knew that this wasn't just an easy fall. Luckily two cars stopped within minutes and both men offered their help, one a former EMT and the other on his way to the hospital where he was working. We were debating if Ashlin should see a doctor but the fact that she felt a little dizzy made the decision very easy and one of the guys, J.R., took her in his car to the ER. The other man, Ross, put her bike on his pickup truck and I cycled to the hospital where we met ten minutes later. Ashlin got a super nice treatment and fortunately we left the ER after only an hour, she with a little glue on her small eyebrow cut and some Band-Aids. We went straight to a motel and used the unplanned free time to relax the sore muscles and to start hopefully fresh tomorrow. Good thing is that we still had some of Laura's homemade beef jerky which will probably give us plenty of power for another day full of cycling tomorrow.

We can only thank J.R., Ross, the ER team and everyone who was super nice to us today.

Day 32 – Blown Away

The typical pattern continues. After the rain there is the wind. We have experienced this phenomenon quite often in the last weeks that a strong headwind is blowing in our face after we had a day of rain before. We have a lot of time to think about that while riding our bicycles but we still haven't figured it out yet. Maybe a meteorologist is reading this and can explain it to us. We had 15mph wind in our face the whole day and I guess this would be similar to cycling an extra 10-15 miles in addition to our impressive 65 miles today. Kansas also doesn't offer much to block the wind since the landscape is characterized by a lot of flat farmland. But is The Sunflower State really so flat? Almost everyone would probably say yes and argue that it's definitely under the Top 5 of the flattest states of the United States BUT IS IT??? What if I told you that you won't find it under the Top 5 and here starts the interactive part of this book:

Email us at cyclingthewestcoast@gmail.com to let us know what you THINK (not what you google) what the Top 5 flattest states are and if you want to outperform everyone else you can also try to guess the most mountainous state of the US. Good luck.

Day 33 – A Night at the Bike Shop

 A sunny day comes to its end and our spot for tonight couldn't be more perfect than a bike shop. We cycled big time today and arrived in Newton, KS after 75 miles of pedaling. The wind changed direction and gave us a little support so that we arrived in less than six hours with an average of 13mph. It was a pretty lonely ride for us since there were not many cities, villages or even gas stations along the way but you know what, we liked it. We could horse around with the animals along our route (mainly horses ☺) and take some cool pictures. Kansas can be very beautiful and the long endless roads kept fascinating us. The landscape is characterized by a lot of farmland full with cattle or horses and every now and then you can spot some of the horse head oil pumps. For someone like me, who loves cowboy country like Texas, there couldn't be a more beautiful setting. Mid-afternoon we arrived in Newton which has a big Mennonite community so you can't expect a lot to be open on a Sunday but we found Oklahoma based Braums which offers burgers, ice cream and groceries. A weird combination but the burgers and banana splits turned us into big fans. Newton also has a pretty cool bike shop and hosts cyclists in their store. Since it is Sunday we were skeptical if someone would let us in but they take care of cyclists almost 24-7 and we were greeted by Mike who showed us around and cleaned our bikes and made them look like new. Now it's just us in the bike store and we are enjoying amenities like Netflix, kitchen, laundry, beer on tap, an arcade machine and so much more. Life is good and how many of you have ever slept in a bike shop?

Day 34 - Houston, We've Had a Problem Here

No, this is not the second part of Day 25 where I used this headline already but there couldn't be a better day to use this quote again than today. The reason? We were on our 60-mile journey to Sterling, KS when we decided to go to Hutchinson instead. Sterling looked like there was not much going on besides camping in the city park or staying at an expensive motel. There was really nothing else so we went for Hutchinson which meant a shorter day for us BUT the possibility to visit the Cosmosphere which has the original and restored Apollo 13 capsule on display that got into trouble while traveling to the moon. Amazing, isn't it? Besides that, there was a lot to see about the beginnings of the manned spaceflight including many facts and exhibits of the German V2 rocket, developed under Wernher von Braun.

Another reason to choose Hutchinson as the final destination of today's trip was that the Zion Lutheran Church hosts cyclists in their building which means we are enjoying a lot of great amenities again like showers, kitchen, huge beds, dvds and even a piano. Maybe I can learn at least how to play one Katy Perry song ☺

All in all, it was a 45-mile day and that means that we have to go a little longer tomorrow but weather conditions are still looking very favorable and with the "flat" landscape we should be flying through Kansas.

Life is good.

Day 35 – Finding the Needle in the Haystack

 Yep, there was not much more than a lot of haystacks along our way to Larned, KS. At least we were lucky to pass by an exotic animal farm after ten miles. Unfortunately, the owners must be as much interested in generating business as TransAm cyclists in getting a flat because they couldn't organize a tour for us or even let us walk around. Well, we were still able to take some cool shots of zebras, camels, ostriches and peacocks but left pretty soon and were on our 70-mile journey without any services along the way. We were well prepared with muffins, Gatorade and snack bars but the last 20 miles were definitely pretty tough. We used the remote roads to jump around on haystacks along the way and to talk to Mark, a fellow TransAmer who is cycling west to east. In contrast to us self-supported guys, he had his wife who was driving a van and transporting his equipment and gear. We also met another older couple cycling eastbound but they didn't seem interested in any kind of conversation. Both were wearing noise canceling Bose headphones (the big ones) and bandanas instead of helmets. We asked if they needed help but the woman just shook her head and turned away from us. A very weird couple but we still hope that they will arrive at their final destination wherever it may be.

Tomorrow's trip will take us to Dodge City which is also known as "The Cowboy Capital of the World". Guess who is super excited. Martin!!! Yeehaaaaaaw.

Day 36 – Yeehaaaaaaw

First, because we hit the 2,000-mile mark today and second because we made it to Dodge City. After 65 miles of pedaling we rolled into The Cowboy Capital of the World where we already booked tickets to visit the Boot Hill Museum, eat dinner, watch a gunfight and enjoy a variety show. The Boot Hill Museum basically rebuilt Dodge City to like it looked in the late 1800s and you can find a saloon, general store, barber shop and much more at the museum. Interesting fact, boot hill was a common name for the burial grounds of gunfighters, or those who "died with their boots on" and the museum is located on the original location of the Boot Hill Cemetery. Dodge City is not along the official TransAm route so we had to say goodbye to good old Route 76 which guided us from Virginia to Larned, KS. Today it was definitely worth leaving the TransAm route since we wouldn't have seen the Half Way Sign, which marks half the distance between San Francisco and New York, and Dodge City if we had stayed on the 76. Leaving the route also doesn't mean that hospitality and friendliness stops. Quite the contrary since a random person in a car stopped next to us and gave us $20. Thank you Mark from Dodge City, we will add it to our donations for the John Wayne Cancer Foundation.

It was a pretty tough start from Larned where a strong wind from the south blew with 15-20mph in our face. In addition, a huge wave of clouds covered the horizon and was getting closer and closer. Just to make y'all feel better, we always check the weather before we leave and even use tornado warning apps so don't worry about us. The clouds moved over us and the moment they passed we got a tailwind which more or less accompanied us to Dodge City where we went straight to the museum.

The museum is definitely worth visiting. We learned a lot about how Americans killed more than 60 million buffaloes and reduced them to less than a thousand. After that, we got dinner before the fun part of the evening started. First was the gunfight which was a 15-minute entertainment show outside but the highlight was clearly the variety show where the performers even integrated the audience. Folks, I have to warn you: THERE IS PG13 MATERIAL below so don't read further if you are under 13. I also want to underline that we did what we did to support whatever you can imagine: puppies, troops, low-salary performers,… so don't judge us ☺

Life is good. Yeehaaaaaaw.

Day 37 - "Get The Hell Outta Dodge"

 Yep, we had to follow the saying and leave the beautiful Cowboy Capital of the World this morning. Of course, it's hard to top such an experience and so it wasn't a surprise that the 55-mile ride to Garden City didn't really excite us. Seriously, there was nothing really interesting along the way. We just followed US 50/400 all the way to Garden City. Since this is also a popular truck route, we had many trucks passing us throughout the day and we believe there were only empty or full cattle trucks. We couldn't figure out where they were going to or coming from but halfway into our day we cycled through Ingalls which has a huge feed yard. It was actually our second one we saw during the trip and the capacity of this one is said to be 40,000 heads! I guess there were at least 20,000 cows and you can imagine how much smell they produce (apparently ONE cow produces 66-132 gallon of methane gas everyday). Yes, it was that bad and you can only escape very slowly if you are on a bicycle BUT there must be such feed yards, otherwise there wouldn't be such great burger places like Freddy's which we visited today the first time. Donald, who we stayed with in Springfield, actually recommended it to us and he was so right with his recommendation. Thanks!!! The burgers are fantastic and we've had a lot in the last few weeks to compare it to. If you ever see one of their stores, try it out. We probably gained back the 6lbs we lost today, because after 2,000 miles and almost approaching Arizona and California we were pretty sure that we won't need stuff like winter gloves or down jackets so we prepared a package which will probably arrive in San Diego a little bit ahead of us. Now we are ready for our (probably) last night in Kansas because tomorrow's trip will take us to beautiful Colorado. Let's hope that everything works out well and

the 75 miles won't involve too many feed yards ☺
Smell you later!

Day 38 – 104 Miles to Colorado

It's very hard to believe but we hit 100 miles today and finished in Lamar after cycling for 104 miles. We don't know what it was. It could have been the burger from Freddy's yesterday evening which gave us so much power, the espresso this morning, the fact that we were about to cycle into our sixth state Colorado, because we wanted to give Mark Wahlberg an awesome birthday present (Happy Birthday Buddy), or maybe just because we were blessed with an up to 25mph tailwind from the east which carried us through the remainder of Kansas. We even gained an hour and can now say that we are in Mountain Time. It was such a great ride cycling in the heaviest gear and averaging more than 14mph. There were parts where we could cycle 20mph without any big effort. Well, if the weather god gives you this great assist, you have to make sure that you score and since we already "scored" 50 miles at 11am we knew we could easily do another 50.

On our way we met four other TransAm cyclists. Two couples, but just one of them stopped and talked to us for a bit. Barbara and Jerry are heading to Virginia where Barbara is also working for the Virginia Bicycle Federation. We had a nice quick chat and took our typical selfie with them. We wish them the best of luck and hope that they didn't have too much trouble with the wind since they were cycling the opposite direction. One man's trash is another man's treasure.

After 70 miles we finally arrived at Colorado's state border, took our pics and we were off for another 30 miles. Temperatures got up to 96F (35 Celsius) so we got some refreshments at a gas station in Granada where we checked the weather and saw that thunderstorms were rolling into Colorado. Fortunately, we arrived in Lamar

before the big downpour started.
Life is good but let's see how we feel tomorrow.

Day 39 - Rocky Mountains in Sight

Only 80 miles into Colorado and we are already able to spot some kind of mountain far far away at the horizon. Yes, it's the first sign of the mountain range lying ahead of us and to be honest it's fascinating to see the Rocky Mountains. The whole time, be it in Illinois, Missouri or Kansas, it was hard to imagine how far we already got. Also the 2,200 miles is just a number but reaching the mighty Rocky Mountains just feels like a big achievement. In addition, we needed some motivation today. It was clear that the perfect day yesterday with 104.5 miles, tailwind etc. couldn't be topped again and only ten miles into our 57 mile ride the wind started blowing with 15mph into our faces. Our average speed dropped under 10mph and the pedaling got harder and harder. We felt tired and then we realized that we are already above 3,500 ft. elevation which doesn't seem a lot but apparently the oxygen in the air is 14% lower than at sea level. I guess that can make it a little harder. Fortunately, the wind calmed down after our lunch break and we finished in La Junta, CO after five hours of pedaling.

It was also the day of the reunions. Only a few miles into our cycling day we saw a hitchhiker on the side of the road. He looked kind of homeless but we would see him later again. After we got a coffee at a gas station around mile 30 he was sitting there waiting for his next lift. Kind of depressing to see that someone can make it this far too without pedaling or any exercise ☺ He wouldn't remain the only one we would see again. After 20 miles of cycling we stopped at a gas station to grab a coffee but unfortunately it was out of business and we just sat down and had a granola bar. A van pulled over and the driver wanted to get oil from the store but he also couldn't buy anything. Luckily, he found a friendly farmer who gave him some oil but missing oil wasn't his only problem. When we arrived in La Junta we saw the van on the side of the road with two hand-drawn signs: "Need gas" and "Out of gas" ☺

Well, let's hope we won't run out of gas/power on tomorrow's ride which will bring us 75 miles closer to the Rocky Mountains. It might be a boring ride but as long as we can spot funny animals along the way there is always entertainment for us.

Day 40 – 80 Looooooong Miles

Oh man, it was a tough one today and probably one of our longest days since we started 40 days ago. We knew that we would have a 75 mile ride from La Junta to Walsenburg ahead of us WITHOUT any service along the route so we packed food, Gatorade and filled our hydration backpacks for the first time. It started pretty easy and we cycled the first ten miles only with a slight headwind. Unfortunately, this headwind transformed into a very strong and annoying one for the remaining 60 miles. The forecast showed calmer wind for noon but that never happened and once again we learned that the weather clowns don't have any clue what's going to happen in one hour or more. You can be happy if they can forecast the current weather accurately. After 25 miles we met Mizuki from Japan. He was an exchange student in Durango where he started his cycling trip towards Washington DC. He will then fly to LA and cycle from LA back to Durango. Cool way of doing such a trip. Good Luck Buddy!

Eventually we arrived in Walsenburg, CO and we were starving. We checked the local restaurants on Google Maps and found a bunch of places but like the last 40 days, so many businesses are out of business and it's really sad to see this trend throughout the whole country. Be it Kentucky, Illinois or Colorado, the small businesses really suffer and only a few are surviving. I think we saw at least five closed restaurants which were up for sale in Walsenburg. We ended up at a Carl's JR burger place and had our probably 30th burger (We are craving a Schnitzel).

That was not it for today, we still had another 3 ½ miles ahead of us to Lathrop State Park and even in the park we had to cycle another 1 ½ miles to our campsite so that we ended up with 80 miles total and 7:54h of cycling plus we climbed from 4,000 ft. to 6,000 ft. BUT if you can enjoy scenic views like the ones below you easily forget how much you exerted yourself just hours ago.

Day 41 – Time for Vacation

After 2,400 miles and 41 cycling days it's time for a mini vacation which we have definitely earned. We started at the Lathrop State Park this morning where we spent a relaxing night under the stars. The route then took us with a gradual incline from 6,000 ft. to over 9,400 ft. to La Veta Pass which marked our first pass of the trip. It was a more than 8-mile-long incline but much much easier than the Ozarks or Appalachians plus it offered awesome views. From there it was another 40 miles until our final destination but the wind and slight descent supported us so that we finished in just a little bit more than six hours.

Since we didn't have any days without cycling for the last six weeks, we decided that it's time to rest our legs to be ready for the last third of our trip. We couldn't have picked a better spot for a rest day than the Zapata Ranch in Musca, CO. One of Ashlin's friends has been working here for the last three years and invited us to stay at her place. The ranch is such an amazing place with the Rocky Mountains around it, a lot of pastures with horses, cattle and even 2,000 buffalos. Jessie showed us around and eventually we ended the day with delicious bison brisket for dinner while sitting around a fire.

Tomorrow we will use our free time to check out this huge farm and the nearby Great Sand Dunes National Park. Stay duned uhh tuned.

Day 42 – From Cycling to Sand Sledding

 Oh guys, it was a nice feeling of not setting an alarm but sleeping in and resting instead. We got up around 8am and just started super relaxed into our day off. Since the Great Sand Dunes National Park and Preserve is only four miles away from the ranch it was a must to go there. Jessie was so kind to give us her car and off we were heading to the park. You can see the dunes from far away but once you get closer and see the little ant-like dots on the dunes, which are actually people walking on them, you realize that these dunes are huge. We stopped at a gas station before we got there and rented a sand board which is basically a sled for sand dunes and I can tell you it's a lot of fun but also super exhausting since it requires you to walk up the dunes, sled down, walk up again and so on but with the great view of the mountains we had, it was worth all the climbing. Once back we used the time to discover more of the 103,000 acres of Zapata Ranch. We ended up on our favorite pasture with view of the mountains and shared our love with some of the 42 horses.

Now we are feeling ready for the remainder of our adventure. Also thanks to a delicious steak dinner with Jessie we should have plenty of energy to master tomorrow's journey to South Fork (which reminds me of South Fork Ranch and my favorite TV show Dallas) ☺

Life is good and we can still find sand on our bodies.

Day 43 – Back On the Road…

…… or the story of how to rent a full cabin for $57.

It was hard to leave Zapata Ranch this morning after we spent two wonderful days there. The forecast showed rain spread over the whole day and it accompanied us for the first ten miles. Combined with the cracked and bumpy roads it felt even harder to be back on the bikes but the sun came out and followed us on our ride from the ranch to Del Norte where we wanted to grab lunch after our first 45 miles. I also noticed that a screw on my right pedal cage came loose and I wanted to fix it as soon as possible. Fortunately, we found an auto repair shop in Del Norte where Coby, a young boy, was super friendly and assisted me getting the right tools to fix it. Thanks a lot buddy!

We couldn't have timed our lunch break better because the moment we sat down for lunch a rain shower arrived in Del Norte. We used the break to get our usual burger and surprise surprise a cappuccino and a caramel macchiato. It's always a big highlight if we find fancy coffee drinks along the way and this time had an interesting dialogue with David the barista who told us about his 28-day hiking trip in Wyoming. Maybe something the Cycling The West Coast team should focus on after the Transamerica trip??? We only had 17 more miles left and even the headwind couldn't slow us down so that we arrived in South Fork early afternoon. We had booked a room at a motel and cabin place and somehow they couldn't accommodate our booking of a king room without giving us a full cabin incl. fireplace, 2 bedrooms, full kitchen, … Since they also have a hot tub on-site, we could finally relax our muscles and prepare them for the climb up to the Continental Divide tomorrow. The route will take us up to more than 10,000 ft. to Wolf Creek Pass.

Apparently it's the 71st hardest climb in the US out of PJAMM Top 100 but if you are a positive thinker like we are it's actually the 30th easiest out of the 100 ☺
Wish us luck and good weather.

Day 44 – Crossing the Great Divide

Oh yes we did it. It was a 2 ½ hour climb up to almost 11,000 ft. but at 10am we could straddle the Continental Divide. For all those who don't know what the Great or Continental Divide is, it is where all rivers east of it flow into the Atlantic Ocean or Gulf of Mexico (e.g. Rio Grande or Mississippi River) and all river west of the divide will run into the Pacific Ocean. It's kind of a big thing for cyclists since there is no official midpoint of the route, especially not for our adjusted route. You can probably say it's only downhill from here if you find a river which you can follow to the Pacific ☺ We crossed at Wolf Creek Pass and learned that it took two days in a Model-T Ford in 1916 to pass but only if you were lucky and your brakes didn't burn or your radiator didn't boil.

The downhill part was so pretty that we had to use the GoPro to film our way to Pagosa Springs. We stopped at a very scenic lookout and another time to check out Treasure Falls. We soaked in the beautiful landscape which was probably one of the most beautiful along our trip. The chipmunks didn't care very much about the landscape but more about my cereal bar so we shared it generously.

Once in Pagosa Springs we grabbed lunch at the Riff Raff Brewing Company and rewarded ourselves with some brewskis but that was not the only reward. Pagosa Springs is well known for its hot springs and we went straight to a bathhouse to relax in 105F warm geothermal water. The moment we entered the building I was shocked by the smell but learned that it's the sulfur which makes the hot spring water stink like rotten eggs. It's definitely stinky but if it helps…. ☺

Now the best for last. Our timing hasn't always been as

good as today. Often we arrive at cafés or restaurants on their one and only day they are closed but today it was rodeo time in Pagosa Springs and we got to see everything from bull and barrel riding to steer wrestling and mutton busting. To get there we had to walk a mile along a highway with no sidewalk so I asked a guy in a pickup truck if he could give us a ride and he drove us directly to the entrance. He was a Texan and we are thankful that we met him. I guess we will fall asleep with a big smile on our faces tonight.

Yeehaaaaaaw!

PS: At the rodeo we learned that it had snowed at 3:45PM today at Wolf Creek Pass, only five hours after we went over with the sun shining on us.

Day 45 – Free Donuts for Hill Climbers

We left Pagosa Springs early this morning and thought the hills would be a part of our trip history but we couldn't have been more wrong. Right outside of Pagosa we had to pedal 2-3 miles straight up. The view over Pagosa was nice but soon forgotten since we continued our journey. We cycled along good old 160 West and had planned to stop after ~25 miles in Piedra. Unfortunately, the city Piedra seems to be 3-4 houses next to each other so that we totally missed it and only realized that a few miles later. A break and a snack would have been nice but the weather and wind were favorable so we continued our ride which took us directly to the next big climb to over 8,000 ft. We must have looked very exhausted or close to starvation because once we reached the top we noticed a car on the side of the road. Toni and Eddie, a super sweet couple, got out of their car and offered us donuts. Wow, the bicycle god must have heard our prayers for food. We couldn't say no and enjoyed Voodoo Doughnuts while chatting with both.

Lunch time was then in Bayfield which was unspectacular so that we went straight to Suzy and David's place south of Durango. Suzy and David are friends of Ashlin's family and they invited us to their wonderful property. We relaxed in the sun with view of the mountains until they got back from work. They were one of the best hosts and we enjoyed homemade margaritas, beers and Mexican food while watching the sunset over the mountains. We are super thankful that we could hang out with them tonight and the fact that we stayed up pretty late shows you fellow readers how much we enjoyed the time together.

Y'all have a good night and enjoy yourselves now.

Day 46 – Ka-Ching

 We had a very peaceful and relaxing night at Suzy and David's place and started with a yummy breakfast into the day. Since we had to go through Durango, Suzy and David recommended the best route but only moments later we convinced Suzy to ride with us to Durango and enjoy 15 miles of feeling like a TransAmer. She was a great wing woman and navigator and dropped us off close to the city center. We decided to check out her book store and two of the local bicycle shops before we were off to our journey through the mountains. Yep, they are still there and we had a tough climb to >8,000 ft. to Hesperus ahead of us where thick and dark thunderstorm clouds waited for us. We managed to pass them and expected a nice long downhill part but found ourselves back in more uphill climbing after a slight descent. It was definitely a lot of climbing and our fuel was running low when we arrived in Mancos for our lunch break. Suzy's café recommendation delivered as she had promised and we refueled with pasta and lavender lemonade. From there it was only 2 ½ hours until our final destination Towaco but the rain made it feel like four hours. On our way we passed the Mesa Verde National Park. It was a bummer that we couldn't visit it but the steep climbs and narrow roads in the park are not very bicycle friendly. Maybe next time when we visit David and Suzy for their big August party ☺

After 75 miles on the bicycle computer we arrived at the weirdest spot we have slept so far. An Indian casino or am I supposed to say Native American Casino? Well, let's say it's a casino run by the ancestors of people who lived in America before Columbus set a foot on this continent. We are not the biggest gamblers and usually choose the cheapest slot machines with the coolest designs but with

$20 free to play from the casino we were going BIG. The biggest win happened at the Bierhaus slot (I probably don't have to translate that) and we ended up with the promo money in cash in our pockets. Ka-ching. I guess it will be another night where we will fall asleep with a big smile. Unfortunately, it will be our last night in Colorado for a while and as long as nobody from The Centennial State is reading this and offering me a cowboy position at their farm we have to say goodbye for a little bit.

Day 47 – Four Places at Once

Today something weird happened. Usually I start thinking of what to write the moment we begin in the morning but today I seemed distracted and stunned a lot which took away my "free time" to think about the diary. The reason? Well, there was so much happening around us that we almost forgot how hard it can be to cycle 75 miles. We started with an awesome downhill part from the casino which lasted almost twenty miles and didn't require much pedaling. Five miles later we arrived at an intersection where we were about to make a turn but Four Corners was five miles straight and so we cycled to this monument. For all of you who don't know what the Four Corners is, it's the only spot in the USA where four US states border each other at one point so we were able to set our feet and hands in New Mexico, Colorado, Arizona and Utah at the same time. It was pretty busy but we got a few chances to take some pictures and heard that it can get really crazy with long waiting lines. We then had to cycle five miles back to the intersection and from there the lonely part through a stunning landscape begun. We are still miles away from Monument Valley but the landscape already offers great previews. It's a mix of canyons, mountains and the San Juan River, all in a great reddish color and it's amazing how fast the landscape changed. Just one day ago we were cycling through snow covered mountains and pine tree forests and now it's all dry, hot and full of red rocks. Towns are also getting a little scarcer so we now have to load up on food and water whenever we get a chance plus fill our hydration backpacks. Unfortunately, the food choices are still limited and most of the time it's only what gas stations are offering but it doesn't seem like we have lost any weight so far ☺ It might also due to our regular burger for dinner which was also on our menu for tonight. We ended our journey in Bluff, Utah where we found a great café with beautiful views on the Navajo Twins rock formation. From here it's only 48 miles to Monument Valley which we will tackle tomorrow. We are already excited to ride the same way Forrest Gump was running and where he stopped in the movie.

Yeehaaaaaaw from Uuuuuutaaahh

Day 48 – Making the Trip Monumental

We started our journey to Monument Valley from the Kokopelli Inn in Bluff where we were able to relax our muscles from the 75 mile ride yesterday. For all those, who don't know what a Kokopelli is, it's a fertility deity, usually depicted as a humpbacked flute player and who has been venerated by some Native American cultures in the Southwestern United States. It took us 25 miles from the Inn until we saw the first signs of Monument Valley but around mile 32 we got super slow and kept stopping multiple times to take pictures of the breathtaking landscape. We also made it to the spot we mentioned in yesterday's journal entry where Forrest Gump stops running. Of course we had to copy his picture, take elevated photos and just enjoy the views. It was definitely a great idea leaving the official bicycle route 76 and being able to cycle along those sights. We were done around 2pm and pitched our tent at the Goulding campground which offers great amenities like an indoor pool, a lot of showers, laundry and super friendly people. We visited their restaurant just a mile down the road which offers beautiful scenic views over the valley and we enjoyed those for lunch while having ...... NO not a burger but pasta and a club sandwich plus yummy dessert ☺

We also met Andy and his wife Regina and talked to them for a little bit. They are both from Virginia and knew exactly where we were coming from when we mentioned Yorktown, VA. Andy is a police officer and we enjoyed chatting with him and his wife about our trip and his career. There are really great people in this country and many of them have interesting stories to tell. I am usually a very outgoing person and not shy to talk to people but during this trip we even got more out of our comfort zone

98

and talked to all kind of people. For example, at the campground I saw a huge pickup truck pulling a gigantic RV trailer and I always wondered how they are attached to the trucks so I just went to the owners Chris and Jennifer who were happy to show it to me. We can only recommend talking to strangers (btw we don't like the word stranger and that's why we have the quote "A stranger is just a friend you haven't met yet" on our business card) and hear their stories. Try it.

Day 49 – Lucky 7

Yep, it has been seven weeks times seven days we have been on the road right now and there couldn't be a better reason to celebrate this than by entering into our last state before California. It only took us three miles this morning until we arrived in The Grand Canyon State Arizona which reminds me of one of my favorite singers and songs: "I've got some ocean front property in Arizona" sung by George Strait. Well, we can't smell the ocean yet but we are getting closer. Today we "only" got 38 miles closer but only because it would have been another 61 miles from our motel in the middle of nowhere to the next town. A challenge we want to keep for tomorrow. Today's ride took us first to Kayenta where we enjoyed an early lunch, followed by eleven super windy miles to Tsegi or whatever this area or county is called. The wind is also a reason for us to leave early tomorrow in addition to the nice toasty temperatures around 90F. We are still in Navajo Indian Tribe area and those guys must not have a good relationship with AT&T or any other carrier since there is barely reception here.

Day 50 – Turning into Early Birds

After managing thunderstorms and temperatures in the low 40s, it's now time to beat the heat since the thermometer tries to hit the 100F almost everyday. This and the fact that the wind is usually picking up during the course of the day, made us get up at 530AM this morning to leave early. Unfortunately, it's super confusing to determine what time it is. First, we are in Arizona which doesn't have Daylight Savings Time so it would be three hours back compared to New York or same time as California but since we are in Navajo Tribe Country, we still have to follow Mountain Daylight Savings Time. Americans and their time zones are definitely weird. Well, so we got up at 530AM Tribe Time and were on the road before 7AM. Fortunately, the wind and heat were manageable so that we arrived at our final destination Tuba City already at 12pm (also Tribe Time ☺). Our journey didn't include many highlights. The canyons and hills are slowly disappearing and the landscape is changing more and more into a boring desert but that will change tomorrow when we will climb up to the rim of the Grand Canyon. It will be a lot of climbing but the view should be a big motivator for us.

We also ran/cycled into another cyclist today. Shinsuke is on his way from the Santa Monica Pier to New York and gave himself three months to achieve this great adventure. Of course, we will think of him and wish him save travels. Some other encounters we are experiencing in this area are the so called Res Dogs which stands for reservation dogs. These poor guys live around gas stations and motels where they hope to get some food. We met quiet a few the last couple of days and tried to feed them some snacks. Unfortunately, those guys want to take the whole mile after giving them an inch and don't want us to leave them.

If we only had a trailer….

Day 51- Grand Achievement

Again we started very early into the day. Immediately after our breakfast we were on the road at 645AM to tackle our 60-mile trip to the Grand Canyon. We knew that our final destination was at 7200 ft. elevation and once we left Tuba City and cycled two hours more or less downhill to Cameron, we knew that the next 30 miles would be tough and include a lot of low gear pedaling. The good thing was that the shoulder was wide enough and the traffic pretty light but it was a gradual 30-mile incline with temperatures in the high 80s. Our plan was to get to the Desert View campground, which is on the south rim and east side of the Grand Canyon, as early as possible to save a camping spot. Unfortunately, you can't make reservations and it only has 50 campsites on a first come first serve basis so the whole time we were pedaling we didn't know if we would even get a spot. Luckily we gained an hour and are now in the Pacific Time Zone. At 1130AM, following 5 hours and 40 minutes of pedaling, we finally arrived at the campground where we also found a few empty campsites. Phew. After setting up our camp and tent we were craving water and food and cycled half a mile to the general store. The view was not our priority one because we knew it would still be there later so we grabbed some food and drinks and recovered from our exhausting ride. Once we were back to normal, we went to the rim and we must tell you it was gorgeous. I've been to the Grand Canyon once with my parents but I didn't remember it being so breathtaking and beautiful. It almost seems unreal or like a painting because I haven't seen anything similar before. The canyon is so deep and full of different colors that it was worth every mile pedaling. Another big surprise of the Grand Canyon National Park was that you are allowed to drink alcohol everywhere in the park except in the parking lot and inside buildings so we were finally able to cheers at our campsite to more than 2,900 miles. We used the rest of the afternoon to relax and sort our stuff for the last ten days of cycling. We still found a few items we never used and which we ditched.

The highlight of the day was definitely the sunset which we enjoyed from Navajo Point. It was a very peaceful and relaxing atmosphere and just amazing to experience this moment after cycling through almost the whole country. The sunset alone was worth every painful mile and we are so happy that we decided to do this trip. A lot of time we run into people who are retired and started similar trips very late in their life but I can only recommend to anyone who is thinking about such an adventure DON'T WAIT just do it. You won't regret it.

Life is good!

Day 52 - Yabba Dabba Doo to 3.000 Miles

Another day of cycling comes to an end and we can proudly say that we hit the 3,000-mile mark and ended up in Bedrock City at the Flintstone Campground but let me start chronologically. We woke up early, since we were still used to Mountain Daylight Savings Time, and tried to hit the road as soon as possible but somehow it was already 7:30AM when we finally left our campsite. The 25 miles to Grand Canyon Village were simply too beautiful and we stopped many many times to take pictures and enjoy the view so that it was already 1030AM when we finally entered the village. We were hoping for an empty spot at their campground but since it was booked out months in advance when we checked it online, it was not a surprise to find a full campground. Our backup plan was to cycle to Williams which would have been another 55 miles but due to the hot weather and increasing headwind we were looking for alternatives which were rare along the way. It was clear that today wouldn't be an 85+ mile day so we decided to cycle to Valle and check out the campground. The road was pretty empty on our side but full with cars, RVs and trucks on the other. Well, it's Friday and travel season so it's not a surprise to see those thousands of cars going to the Grand Canyon. About seven miles away from Valle we spotted something at the horizon which looked liked a guy pushing a wheelchair on the shoulder but once we got closer it became clear that this was a guy pushing one of those jogging strollers moms and dads use to run with their little kids. We stopped and chatted with him and learned that he started in Florida in March and his final stop was the Grand Canyon. Why? Because he wants to show his 6-year-old son that nothing is impossible. His name was John and we chatted for quite a bit when we realized that he was also pushing a 9 ½-week old German shepherd puppy on his stroller. It was so cute. The stroller was built to handle 100 lbs. max but his load including the dog was closer to 120 lbs. John seemed like a great guy and we would have loved to spend more time with him but we both had to move/walk/cycle on. Seven miles later we arrived at the campground which also features a Flintstone Park you can visit. Our priority was water, shower, food and rest and we found all of it at the campground.

Tomorrow we will try to leave even earlier and hit the road around sunrise to enjoy pedaling in temperatures below 80 as long as possible.

Yabba Dabba Doo!

Day 53 - 100+100=4x4

 Ha, I guess only a few people might get this formula after reading it so let me quickly explain. First, we hit another 100 miles today but it wasn't an easy day since temperatures quickly went above 90F and reached 100F during the course of the day. It didn't even matter that we left at 530AM because temperatures were already in the 80s only two hours later. Luckily the route was not too bad. After 30 miles of pedaling we arrived in Williams where we had to go on the Interstate 40 for 15 miles. Now, it actually sounds scarier than it really is. It's basically like cycling on a regular state road, just that there are more trucks but luckily the shoulder is much bigger and in better condition. There was also no alternative and both the maps we use and Google Maps directed us via the interstate. It was a perfect ride since it was mostly downhill and we were off it faster than it took us to get there. We rewarded ourselves with a nice breakfast in Ash Fork, the least we deserved after cycling 47 miles by 930AM. From there it was a hot ride along the US 89 and we must say it was definitely not a very beautiful one. The shoulder quality was mixed and we were also surprised how many pickup trucks got pretty close to us, most of them on purpose in our opinion. Well, we made it to Prescott which we only chose because it would give us the opportunity to enjoy one of the best burgers in the US at In-N-Out. It was worth the 100 mile trip and we both enjoyed a 4×4 burger which stands for four burger patties and four slices of cheese ☺ Even after 52 days and many of them with at least one burger nothing can compete against an In-N-Out burger.
Now it's time to digest.

Day 54 – Happy Father's Day

Yes, even on our trip we are still able to follow the calendar and know which day of the week or which holiday it is so we decided to use this holy day to show our love to all daddies around the world by not cycling today. Well, it was also mainly because we got our first flat tire yesterday after riding over a big metal piece on the shoulder. Fortunately, we are in Prescott which has a few bicycle shops but only one or two open on Sundays and not before 10AM. It would have been a hot cycling day if we had started around lunch time so we decided to check out the historic downtown area and relax our muscles after our 100 miles yesterday. The tire was fixed pretty quickly and we spent the day walking through Prescott. It's a very neat city with a lot of restaurants, cafés and a beautiful park around the courthouse. Prescott is also the birthplace of the rodeo. On July 4th 1888 local businessmen and merchants organized the first "cowboy tournament" which evolved into the rodeo as which we know it today including bull riding, barrel racing and steer wrestling. Unfortunately, there weren't any rodeos scheduled for tonight so that we only checked out the local western stores and relaxed in the park. A culinary highlight was definitely the local brewery were we tasted flights of beer for lunch. We are also in the final planning phase of our trip since it looks like we will arrive at the west coast next weekend. It still feels unreal that we will be done so soon and it's probably getting even weirder the closer we get. Looking back, it seems like a super long time that we rode our bicycles through states like Virginia and Kentucky but it's still the same amazing adventure it has been the last 54 days. Now we need to focus on the remaining 400 miles which will probably be a little hotter than the 3,100 before ☺

Happy Father's Day and cheers to all daddies.

Day 55 – Hot, Hotter, Wickenburg

 Another day, another chance for the temperatures to hit the 100F and it didn't take long until we had a toasty 104F. Fortunately, we left Prescott at 7AM and had the protection of the Prescott National Forest for our first hour of cycling which went straight up to 6,100 ft. It seemed weird to us that there are still pretty high hills in this part of the country but it didn't take long and we were on a downhill ride for more than fifteen miles. The view of the valley while cycling down was very beautiful but also showed us what is lying ahead of us – a lot of flat and hot desert-like land. We ran into Bob, a 73-year-old cyclist who was on his 20-mile morning ride. It was very impressive to see him cycling up the hill so fast considering he was also recovering from bronchitis.

Only three hours into our day we already had 35 miles on our bicycle computers and decided to stop for a coffee break in Yarnell. For a city with 750 people they surprised us with a great coffee place. The Shearer Delite had lattes and espressos of any kind and we refueled for the remaining 25 miles. Refueling wouldn't have been necessary since it was almost completely downhill to our final stop Wickenburg. Even the warm wind couldn't slow us down but it definitely dried us out. You can compare it with cycling while putting a hair dryer in front of your face for the whole time.

That was also the reason that we picked a hotel for tonight and didn't go outside before sunset. We used the time to go through our whole trip and it's funny to see that there are cities we don't really remember anymore. Good thing we have it all written down.

Tomorrow's trip won't bring us lower temperatures but it should be another day of more downhill than uphill and "only" 55 miles of cycling. You can guess when we will hit the road – Yep EARLY!

Day 56 – Only Cacti and us

 Hello you lucky guys enjoying temperatures under 100F and lower highs than our lows. We are in the middle of the heat wave and I referred to a hair dryer in our faces yesterday but today it felt more like putting your face close to a bonfire. Good thing we expected this heat and were on the road around 630AM. Google Maps showed a little bit more than four hours of cycling and was accurate as always because at 1130AM we sat down in a cool restaurant in Salome, AZ which marked the final destination of our day. Guess what was on the menu. Yep, a beef patty with some veggie deco between a bun accompanied by some potato products ☺ Same old same old but we try to enjoy the fact that we will burn all the calories in the remaining four cycling days if everything works out as planned. Isn't that crazy? It still feels like we are far away from the coast with its nice fresh breezes but it's "only" 260 more miles. It won't be much colder for the rest of the trip so we will keep getting up early and enjoy temperatures in the 80s as long as possible.

Today's route was a straight line from Wickenburg to Salome and the road was empty and seemed to disappear at the horizon due to the glimmering heat. I think it won't take very long until we start seeing mirages of camels and oases at the horizon. At least we got to see a lot of cacti today (plural of cactus) and these so called saguaro are really amazing. The tallest one is around 45ft and they can live for 150-200 years. There are also a lot of laws in place to protect these poky desert trees but I couldn't find one forbidding me to hug them. Those were also the only highlights along our way today so that I won't waste your valuable time much longer. There might be more to tell tomorrow when we will set our feet and tires into CALIFORNIA!!!

Day 57 – California Here We Come

 We did it!!! After 57 days on the road, today was the day we finally made it to our last state. Although there are still 220 miles ahead of us, it felt like a great achievement after cycling 3,100 miles through nine other states in a little bit more than eight weeks. The hot temperatures followed us and we arrived in Blythe when the thermometer showed 105F. Fortunately, we found a nice cafe with the green mermaid in their logo and used the break to cool down before heading to our motel. Even if we had looked for a campground, it would have been simply too hot to camp so we are going to use the comfort and air conditioning of motels for the last days. The motel served also a good spot to check out my bike. The back tire showed a little bit of tear at some spots and it seemed to be caused by the heat, road conditions and of course the thousands of miles, but to be honest I would have expected for them to last for the whole trip. Since Ashlin got already a new back tire, we decided to switch mine too and be prepared for a long ride tomorrow. Once the back tire was put back together, we noticed that there was a tiny little metal piece stuck in the old tire and only a couple of hours later we had to replace the old tube in the new tire too. It might have happened on the I-10 today while cycling on the shoulder. It's really sad, disappointing and disgusting to see how much garbage, especially tire pieces, lay on or next to the shoulder. Well, the rest of the trip should be off the major highways so that we hope we can make it to the coast with our new tires and without any flats.

Tomorrow's trip will take us to Brawley and through a long stretch of remote desert. We will make sure that we are carrying enough water and snacks.

Day 58 - In the Sahara

Oh boy, what a day. We started into our day at 5AM and the sun was not even up by then but temperatures were already in the 80s. The first 20 miles took us from Blythe to Palo Verde along pastures and farmland and we were happy that we chose Blythe over Palo Verde to stay the night before. We would have saved 20 miles today but Palo Verde definitely would have been a bad choice. Except for their gas station, they didn't have anything there and almost everything was out of business. Also the road turned into a rough asphalt mix which probably slowed us down by 1-2 mph. Not much but on an eight-hour day good road conditions can save you a lot of time. The road went uphill for 25 miles and included a lot of rolling hills and the fact that we had to cycle 88 miles was constantly in our minds. We tried to imagine it as a 45-mile day since the elevation profile showed only downhill from mile 45. Unfortunately, this was also a mix of rolling hills and windy flatlands which wouldn't make us go faster than 13 miles per hour. In addition, the heat was really drying us out. We were well prepared and also got lucky at the top of the hill where border patrol officers refilled our water bottles. The next and only stop before Brawley was Glamis and we found a store on the map. We were skeptical because we read on other cyclist's blogs that it was closed. The luck was with us and it was open and we were able to get some snacks and water. A few people asked about what we are usually eating during the course of the day and we can only say that it always depends on the kind of stores along the way. Before we got to Arizona we could find restaurants and stores almost every 20-30 miles but on a day like today we only had this one and only store. It meant that it was water, sodas and ice cream for lunch. Yummy :-/

From there the landscape changed dramatically. We crossed the North Algodones Dunes Wilderness Area and it looked like we were in the Sahara. Approaching cars and trucks blew sand in our faces and the sunscreen made it stick to our whole bodies. Around 2pm we finally cycled into Brawley and felt super relieved. We found a motel and tried to relax for tomorrow's trip to Julian. It will include a long climb to 4,500 ft. towards the end of the day and also mark the real last challenging trip day. It's like at the Tour de France where the the overall Tour standings are typically settled before the final stage and the last day is used to drink champagne while cycling along the Champs D'Élysées. That's our plan for the day after tomorrow when we will hopefully have our real last day.

Day 59 – It's the Final Countdown

Another great song and a perfect description of where we are right now – in Julian, CA very very close to the finish line. Julian experienced a gold rush in the past but its hallmark is now apple pie which we had to try of course. But first we had to earn our pies and to get here we had to master our last challenging climb which took us up to almost 4,500 ft. This elevation gain should help us tomorrow on our way down to the Pacific Ocean. All in all, it was a 73-mile day which started pretty flat and fast for about 40 miles and then went up step by step. In contrast to yesterday's trip through the desert we expected a few more stores or gas stations along the way but couldn't find any and eventually we had to go to a closed campground to refill our water bottles at its restrooms. We still had some food leftovers which helped us through the day but we also felt the exhaustion from yesterday's 92 mile ride. After 64 miles, we took another break on the side of the road, lay down and prepared ourselves mentally for the last eight miles of climbing. I said how funny it would be if there was a store just 500ft from where we took our break and once we were back on our bikes it was not 500 but maybe 1,000 ft. until we saw a store where we immediately stopped again. The one and only store and we lay down 1,000ft away from it ☺
From there the ice cream, Gatorade and water helped us to finish after seven hours of cycling. The reward was a big sandwich, quesadillas and of course apple pie ☺
So what's going on tomorrow? Well, it won't be different than any other cycling day except that we will be DONE!

Day 60 – The End?

Yes, it's true. After 3,519 miles we arrived in Solana Beach where we finally put our front tires in the Pacific Ocean. It was a 60-day journey through Virginia, Kentucky, Illinois, Missouri, Kansas, Colorado, New Mexico, Utah, Arizona and California which took us more than 300 hours of cycling and through three different time zones but first let us tell you what happened today.

Today's trip was more or less a steady downhill journey from Julian to Solana Beach. With an elevation drop of almost 5,000 ft. it didn't cost us so much effort to arrive at Ashlin's parents house where we were greeted with Prosecco, a very creative drawing at their gate, coffee and of course a lot of hugs. From there it was only five miles to the beach but it already felt like we achieved our target and since we were not in a rush, we took our time. Eventually we headed to the beach and I am happy that my parents could also join for the final mile via Skype. They made me who I am and I am happy to have them. After we arrived at the ocean, we had to put our front tires into the Pacific Ocean which marked the official end of our TransAm trip. We took more pictures and even attracted Nashville musician Jeffrey James who wanted to take a picture WITH US. (I always thought it's the other way around ☺) After that we headed home and just relaxed for the rest of the day from our trip.

Would we do it again? Definitely. It was such a great experience and we had the chance to see parts of this country which are off the typical roads and sights and we enjoyed every minute. We are glad that we met so many people who shared their amazing stories with us and that we received so much friendliness and hospitality. We were invited to stay at people's houses, got free food and drinks and a lot of motivational feedback. It has been challenging multiple times and to motivate yourself each day to get back on the bike no matter what temperatures are outside or how much rain is pouring down is not easy but we were lucky to have each other and help us through any kind of pain. If we only inspired a handful of people to do something similar it has been worth every mile of cycling. We can only encourage you to focus on what makes you happy and of how much time you own while doing your job (thanks for this quote Donald). The one book who inspired me the most was The Happiness Advantage written by Shawn Achor and it was a big driver behind my action of quitting my job and going on this trip. We didn't train for this and there is no way you can train for such an adventure. It's a learning curve but it was so much fun to move up this curve everyday. We met many TransAmers and the age gap reached from 21 to over 70 so there is no reason why you wouldn't be able to do it too. We want to thank everyone who followed, supported, helped, motivated, accompanied and inspired us during the last 60 days. It would take too long to thank each individual here and there were so many people who helped us even with little things like giving directions or waving at us. We can only say "You guys rock." and keep up this great attitude. Will this be the end of this our bicycle stories? Probably not. There will be more to come in the next coming days. Stay tuned and excited.

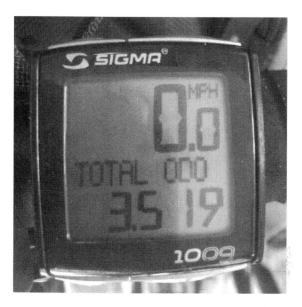

Day 1 Extra - Yo No Hablo Español.

After only four days of rest the cycling fever came back and it was time for another adventure. Unfortunately, I had to fly solo this time because my wing woman Ashlin is still in recovery mode and enjoying the life of a non-cyclist. I decided to take a chance and cycle to a different country since Mexico is "only" 45 miles away. The packing routine this morning was similar to the one on our cross country trip. However, this time there was no need for all the bags, camping stuff etc. so I just took a few repair items, water and some snacks with me in my former handlebar bag which got transformed into a back rack bag since the plastic inside broke. The clock showed 6:20AM when I left and I calculated four hours of cycling to San Ysidro where thousands of Mexicans try to cross into the US everyday.

My route took me along Torrey Pines, La Jolla and Mission Beach until I made it to Old Town San Diego, a neat part of San Diego with a lot of restaurants and bars. Since it was too early for a drink I quickly made it through this district and arrived in downtown only 20-30 minutes later where I stopped at one of the coolest sights of SD – the USS Midway. From there the highlights got scarcer and after passing quite a lot naval bases I found myself on the Bayshore Bikeway which almost brought me all the way to the end. Once at the border I followed the signs and got into Mexico faster than you can say Arriba Arriba. It reminded me a little bit of my journeys from Germany to Poland. You can't read anything, understand anyone and everything looks a little bit run down and busier but there was no reason to feel scared at all. I cycled a couple of miles through the city and was probably the only cyclist in the whole city. Nevertheless, cars were super respectful and even in a huge roundabout everyone maneuvered peacefully around the other. My idea was to try out a Mexican Starbucks but the road seemed to allow cars only so I decided to grab some flan from a local vendor. She didn't understand English but we managed to close a $3 for two items deal. The moment I sat down to enjoy my two treats a man approached me and spoke something in Spanish while rubbing his belly. I assumed he would be hungry but after I said "Yo no hablo español" he said "I also have a bicycle but I am too fat to ride it" while rubbing his belly again. From there the fun was over and I walked back to the border where I waited TWO hours in line to get back to 'Merica. Online it said 30-45 minutes but I guess these are Mexican minutes. Luckily Ash and her mom decided to pick me up behind the border so that it was a very relaxing drive back home.

Buenas Noches!

Route Details

Day 1: Yorktown, VA to Willis Utd. Methodist Church, VA
63.2 Miles, 5h51min
Elevation Gain: 614ft, Elevation Loss -486ft

Day 2: Willis Church, VA to Mineral, VA
73.8 Miles, 6h47min
Elevation Gain 1181ft, Elevation Loss: -843ft

Day 3: Mineral, VA to Charlottesville, VA
45 Miles, 4h28min
Elevation Gain 1411ft, Elevation Loss: -1417ft

Day 4: Charlottesville, VA to Waynesboro, VA
38.7 Miles, 4h38min
Elevation Gain 2093ft, Elevation Loss: -1266ft

Day 5: Waynesboro, VA to Lexington, VA
50.1 Miles, 5h1min
Elevation Gain 1804ft, Elevation Loss: -2028ft

Day 6: Lexington, VA to Daleville, VA
48.3 Miles, 4h49min
Elevation Gain 2047ft, Elevation Loss: -1827ft

Day 7: Daleville, VA to Dublin, VA
72.3 Miles, 7h18min
Elevation Gain 2566ft, Elevation Loss: -1759ft

Day 8: Dublin, VA to Marion, VA
58.3 Miles, 5h17min
Elevation Gain 2270ft, Elevation Loss: -2178ft

Day 9: Marion, VA to Council, VA
56.1 Miles, 5h40min
Elevation Gain 4741ft, Elevation Loss: -5016ft

Day 10: Council, VA to Breaks Interstate Park, VA
34.4 Miles, 4h5min
Elevation Gain 1680ft, Elevation Loss: -1772ft

Day 11: Breaks Interstate Park, VA to Hindman, KY
67.3 Miles, 6h21min
Elevation Gain 3255ft, Elevation Loss: -3996ft

Day 12: Hindman, KY to Booneville, KY
68.9 Miles, 6h14min
Elevation Gain 4291ft, Elevation Loss: -4636ft

Day 13: Booneville, KY to Berea, KY
59.2 Miles, 5h37min
Elevation Gain 3353ft, Elevation Loss: -3041ft

Day 14: Berea, KY to Harrodsburg, KY
50.1 Miles, 4h48min
Elevation Gain 1532ft, Elevation Loss: -1696ft

Day 15: Harrodsburg, KY to New Haven, KY
68.7 Miles, 6h10min
Elevation Gain 1765ft, Elevation Loss: -2142ft

Day 16: New Haven, KY to Mammoth Cave, KY
70.1 Miles, 6h14min
Elevation Gain 1847ft, Elevation Loss: -1581ft

Day 17: Mammoth Cave, KY to Sonora, KY
42.8 Miles, 3h41min
Elevation Gain 1768ft, Elevation Loss: -1785ft

Day 18: Sonora, KY to Falls of Rough, KY
50.6 Miles, 4h20min
Elevation Gain 1542ft, Elevation Loss: -1785ft

Day 19: Falls of Rough, KY to Sebree, KY
69.4 Miles, 6h11min
Elevation Gain 2221ft, Elevation Loss: -2323ft

Day 20: Sebree, KY to Elizabethtown, IL
67.4 Miles, 6h19min
Elevation Gain 2382ft, Elevation Loss: -2405ft

Day 21: Elizabethtown, IL to Carbondale, IL
68.3 Miles, 6h24min
Elevation Gain 1119ft, Elevation Loss: -1063ft

Day 22: Carbondale, IL to Chester, IL
51.2 Miles, 4h29min
Elevation Gain 984ft, Elevation Loss: -728ft

Day 23: Chester, IL to Farmington, MO
48.2 Miles, 4h38min
Elevation Gain 1586ft, Elevation Loss: -1290ft

Day 24: Farmington, MO to Ellington, MO
60.9 Miles, 5h18min
Elevation Gain 2149ft, Elevation Loss: -2398ft

Day 25: Ellington, MO to Houston, MO
71.9 Miles, 6h36min
Elevation Gain 4154ft, Elevation Loss: -3652ft

Day 26: Houston, MO to Marshfield, MO
67.3 Miles, 5h59min
Elevation Gain 2654ft, Elevation Loss: -2345ft

Day 27: Marshfield, MO to Springfield, MO
28.7 Miles, 2h16min
Elevation Gain 387ft, Elevation Loss: -568ft

Day 28: Springfield, MO to Everton, MO
45 Miles, 4h2min
Elevation Gain 407ft, Elevation Loss: -654ft

Day 29: Everton, MO to Pittsburg, KS
65.5 Miles, 5h14min
Elevation Gain 1411ft, Elevation Loss: -1584ft

Day 30: Pittsburg, KS to Chanute, KS
57.9 Miles, 4h25min
Elevation Gain 476ft, Elevation Loss: -463ft

Day 31: Chanute, KS to Chanute, KS
8.6 Miles, 0h48min
Elevation Gain 0ft, Elevation Loss: 0ft

Day 32: Chanute, KS to Eureka, KS
64.5 Miles, 5h32min
Elevation Gain 1450ft, Elevation Loss: -1319ft

Day 33: Eureka, KS to Newton, KS
76.9 Miles, 5h54min
Elevation Gain 1076ft, Elevation Loss: -719ft

Day 34: Newton, KS to Hutchinson, KS
45.3 Miles, 3:24min
Elevation Gain 315ft, Elevation Loss: -223ft

Day 35: Hutchinson, KS to Larned, KS
70.8 Miles, 5h24min
Elevation Gain 482ft, Elevation Loss: -13ft

Day 36: Larned, KS to Dodge City, KS
64.3 Miles, 5h10min
Elevation Gain 581ft, Elevation Loss: -89ft

Day 37: Dodge City, KS to Garden City, KS
54.8 Miles, 4h34min
Elevation Gain 719ft, Elevation Loss: -374ft

Day 38: Garden City, KS to Lamar, CO
104.5 Miles, 7h2min
Elevation Gain 1040ft, Elevation Loss: -256ft

Day 39: Lamar, CO to La Junta, CO
57.4 Miles, 5h13min
Elevation Gain 597ft, Elevation Loss: -144ft

Day 40: La Junta, CO to Walsenburg, CO
79.9 Miles, 7h54min
Elevation Gain 2792ft, Elevation Loss: -696ft

Day 41: Walsenburg, CO to Zapata Ranch, CO
68.9 Miles, 6h28min
Elevation Gain 3743ft, Elevation Loss: -2159ft

Day 42: Zapata Ranch, CO to Zapata Ranch, CO
Rest Day

Day 43: Zapata Ranch, CO to South Fork, CO
63.3 Miles, 5h14min
Elevation Gain 673ft, Elevation Loss: -217ft

Day 44: South Fork, CO to Pagosa Springs, CO
43 Miles, 3h59min
Elevation Gain 2966ft, Elevation Loss: -4139ft

Day 45: Pagosa Springs, CO to Durango, CO
59.3 Miles, 4h57min
Elevation Gain 3169ft, Elevation Loss: -3760ft

Day 46: Durango, CO to Ute Mountain Casino, CO
74.7 Miles, 6h4min
Elevation Gain 2897ft, Elevation Loss: -3720ft

Day 47: Ute Mountain Casino, CO to Bluff, UT
77.4 Miles, 6h36min
Elevation Gain 2208ft, Elevation Loss: -3545ft

Day 48: Bluff, UT to Monument Valley, UT
51.8 Miles, 5h8min
Elevation Gain 3330ft, Elevation Loss: -2316ft

Day 49: Monument Valley, UT to Kayenta, AZ
38.4 Miles, 3h37min
Elevation Gain 1414ft, Elevation Loss: -502ft

Day 50: Kayenta, AZ to Tuba City, AZ
62.8 Miles, 4h31min
Elevation Gain 955ft, Elevation Loss: -2215ft

Day 51: Tuba City, AZ to Grand Canyon, AZ
62.1 Miles, 5h52min
Elevation Gain 3901ft, Elevation Loss: -1404ft

Day 52: Grand Canyon, AZ to Bedrock City Campground, AZ
57.3 Miles, 4h44min
Elevation Gain 961ft, Elevation Loss: -2428ft

Day 53: Bedrock City, AZ to Prescott, AZ
106.6 Miles, 9h34min
Elevation Gain 3127ft, Elevation Loss: -3747ft

Day 54: Prescott, AZ to Prescott, AZ
Rest Day

Day 55: Prescott, AZ to Wickenburg, AZ
62.1 Miles, 4h54min
Elevation Gain 2264ft, Elevation Loss: -5581ft

Day 56: Wickenburg, AZ to Salome, AZ
55.3 Miles, 4h29min
Elevation Gain 692ft, Elevation Loss: -876ft

Day 57: Salome, AZ to Blythe, CA
61.4 Miles, 4h54min
Elevation Gain 1010ft, Elevation Loss: -2618ft

Day 58: Blythe, CA to Brawley, CA
92.4 Miles, 8h26min
Elevation Gain 1181ft, Elevation Loss: -1558ft

Day 59: Brawley, CA to Julian, CA
73.6 Miles, 7h15min
Elevation Gain 4545ft, Elevation Loss: -245ft

Day 60: Julian, CA to Solana Beach, CA
59.6 Miles, 4h35min
Elevation Gain 845ft, Elevation Loss: -5033ft

Stats

Total Miles: 3,519

Average Miles per day: 58.6

Total Cycling Time: 311h 55min

Average Cycling Time per day: 5h 12min

Average pace: 11.3mph

Cumulative Elevation Gain: 108,623ft

(~3.75 times Mount Everest)

Gear List
(You can download the complete list on
www.cyclingthewestcoast.com/bookbonus)

Clothing

Bike Shorts
*Two per person. Three would have been better since
washing was only possible every 2-3 days.*
Jersey
Three jerseys per person.
Socks
*Short cycling socks and long merino wool socks for cold
days and nights.*
Helmet and Cover
*Giro Bishop Helmet without additional cover. You get
wet anyways.*
Gloves
Specialized Geometry Gloves
Shoes
We both wore sandals.
Sandals
*Getting the Northside Burke was the right decision.
Dried quickly and kept our feet cool during warm days.*
Rain Cover for Shoes
*We recommend getting 2 disposable shower caps in a
motel. They'll do the job.*
Arm Warmers + UV Protection
*A pair of UV arm sleeves warmed our arms and
protected them from the sun.*
Buff
*Especially on long and cold downhill parts the Buff
would protect our faces from icy winds.*
Jacket
*We carried Patagonia jackets for cold nights but sent
them home once we got closer to the desert.*

Rain Pants
We each had one pair.

Hat
I love baseball hats so I brought 2 and bought 1 along the way :)

Sunglasses & Straps
Look for ones with good UV protection. In addition, sunglasses will protect you from the wind.

Pants
Zip-Off pants are the best invention ever. We got one pair each and loved them.

Underwear
2 pairs for the time you don't wear bike shorts.

Sports Bra
2 sport bras for Ashlin

Short Sleeve Shirts
2 shirts to go out for dinner or to sleep in.

Swim Trunks/Bikini
You never know when you have the chance to jump into a pool etc.

Shorts
Zip-Off Pants (see above)

Cycling Gear

Bike

Trek 520. A perfect companion for bicycling across America.

Rear Panniers

Each of us had two Axiom Seymour Panniers on our bike rack. They did an awesome job.

Front Panniers/Handlebar Bag

We got Ibera Handelbar Bags. Don't overload them. They can't hold a lot but have a nice see-through pocket for maps.

Cycling Computer

Cateye Bicycle Computer

Water Bottles

2 on each bike

Water Bottle Cages

2 on each bike

Mini Pump

1 on each bike.

Topeak Allen Multi Tool

A MUST for small repairs. 26 tools total.

Mini Cassette Lockring Tool/Hypercracker

Got it because some touring cyclists mentioned it. We never used it and we think you won't either.

Tubes

Check twice if you have the right size and valve. We carried Schrader valves and had Presta on our bikes :)

Tube Repair Kit

Since we only got 2 flats, we changed the tubes to new ones but we would always have 1 or 2 kits with us.

Spare Tires

We brought one foldable spare tire. It takes up a lot of space but might save you.

Chain Lube

We lubed every ~200 miles or after heavy rain.

Brake Cable
You don't want to end up with only one working brake, so better get one of these.

Derailleur Cable
More complicated to install then brake cables but you don't want to be stuck in only 1 gear if your cable breaks.

Chains
We carried one extra chain and didn't have to replace ours at all. We would have a mechanic check the chains every 1,000 miles.

Brake Blocks/Pads
We replaced the pads at least 3 times since they were worn down after long downhill sessions.

Front Light
We never cycled in the dark but it helps to be visible in foggy or rainy conditions.

Rear Light
see above

Chain Maintenance/Rag
A rag to clean the bike/chain.

Bike Lock
We carried two spiral locks and two loop cables with two Master Locks (no keys required)

Pannier Lock
We used the loop cables to secure the panniers.

Spokes, Nipples, Nuts, Bolts, Links, Pins (Chain)
Some bike maintenance stuff we carried but didn't use.

Fiber Fix Spoke
A backup for a broken spoke but in our opinion not important.

Zip Ties
Always helpful.
Duct Tape
Put some of it around a pen. Like zip ties, duct tape is always helpful.
Tire Lever
Extremely helpful if you want to change a tube.
Tire Boot/Patch
In case you have a big hole in your tire and can't replace it. Alternatively, use a dollar bill.

Camping

Tent
We used the Ledge Scorpion 2 Person Tent and loved its value for money. Size was okay. Weight perfect and price a bargain.

Sleeping Bag
Featherlite categorized 20F but we felt a little cold once temperatures dropped to under 40F.

Tarp
Protects your tent from stones, moisture, etc. Get one at Home Depot.

Sleeping Pad
We used air mattresses but blowing them up was a pain. We would recommend paying more for a self-inflating pad.

Sleeping Liner
To give you additional insulation during cold nights. We never used them.

Knife, Fork, Spoon
Necessities for camping.

Cups & Pan
See above. Our pan was tiny and could maybe hold one egg :)

Cooking Stove
We loved our Etekcity cooking stove which made us the perfect espresso every morning.

Gas
You don't want to run out of it :)

Lighter
Our stove had an ignition but we didn't want to rely on that.

Towel
Camping Microfiber Towel

Pocket Knife
In case you are getting attacked by a squirrel :)

Water Filtration
We carried POTABLE AQUA PA+Plus Water Purification but never used it.

Bungee Cables
3 per person. Perfect to tighten the bags on your bike rack.

Zip Lock Bags
Kept some of our stuff dry.

Rope
Never used it.

Storage Bags
Some plastic bags to separate dirty from clean clothing etc.

Camelbak
For long and hot days. We used them a lot once we got to Utah, Arizona and California.

Dry Bag
A 30L dry bag protected our sleeping bags and air mattresses from getting wet.

Toiletries

Razor
I didn't shave for the full bike trip but Ashlin did :)
Soap
Always available at motels but not at campgrounds.
Toothbrush
1 per person
Toothpaste
1 per person
Deodorant
For the times you don't have clean clothing :)
Cream
Hands and face can dry out a lot during a sunny or windy day.
Hand Sanitizer
Always helpful.
Drugs: Advil, Neosporin, Claritin
Whatever makes you cycle faster :)
Salt/Electrolytes
To replenish your reserves.
Sunscreen
It can get very hot and sunny in parts of the country.
Insect Repellent/Tick Remover
We encountered mosquitoes and flies occasionally, but no ticks
First Aid Kit
Luckily, we didn't have to use it.
Anti Diarrhea
Luckily, we didn't have to use it.
Rubber Gloves
For dirty work on your bike.
Toilet Paper
Sometimes, the next bathroom is many miles away...
Sleeping Mask + Ear Plugs
For noisy and bright environments like some campgrounds.
1 Nail Clipper

ChapStick
1 per person
Dental Floss
Butt Butter against chafing
We hope you won't need it but most people do. So did we.
Q-Tips
A handful
1 Small Mirror
Sewing Kit
For small repairs
Feminine Hygiene Products
Necessary for women.
Detergent
A few Tide pods don't take away much space.

Electronics

iPad
Never used it, so we sent it home after a few weeks into the trip.
iPhone
Good for navigation, motel booking, Warm Showers etc.
iPhone charger
1 per person
GoPro
We took some cool pictures with it.
1 GoPro Charger
GoPro Stick/Accessories
Helmet Mount worked best for us.
GoPro Battery
2 extra batteries
Kindle
We were so tired that we never read after a day of cycling, so we also sent it home.
Camera
Not necessary but a good camera definitely beats an iPhone.
Solar Charger
Pretty big and a little heavy but provided us with fully charged phones quite a few times. Easy to strap on your bags.
Mobile Charger
For the times you don't have electricity.
Flashlight
Almost every phone has one.

Radio
Never used it, so we sent it home after a few weeks into the trip.
Speakers
To listen to music on lonely roads.
Memory Cards
In case you are taking too many pictures.
Cycling Computer Battery
We never had to replace one.

Food/Accessories/Other

Insurance
Check your health insurance!
Driver's License
Not only for the beer after a day of cycling.
Credit Card
We rarely needed cash. Thank you VISA.
Pepper Spray/Air Horn
In case flea bags are chasing you. Pepper spray worked pretty well, horn not so much.
Ready Meals
Mountain House offers a great variety of good meals.
Drink Mix/ Gatorade/Nuun
In case you need some flavor in your water.
Flags
Show a little patriotism along your trip.
Pictures
Missing family? Pictures help.
Business Cards
A great way of giving people your phone number or blog.
Snack/Trail Mix
For hungry moments.
Journal+Pen
Because you won't remember everything and in case you want to write a bike touring blog.
Clothes Pin/Safety Pins
For small repairs
Wallet
1 per person
Quarters
For the Laundromat
Hot Cocoa/Coffee/Tea
Perfect after a cold night in a tent.

Mini Espresso Maker
Best invention ever (like Zip-Off pants).
Coffee Ground
For the coffee maker.
Maps
We used Adventure Cycling Association Maps to find our way along the Transamerica Bicycle Trail.

Author's Note

Thank you for joining us in telling the story of how we cycled across America. We hope the friendliness of strangers and the beauty of this country have touched your soul the same way they touched ours.

If you loved the book and have a minute to spare, we would really appreciate a short review on Amazon.

Reviews from readers like you make a huge difference in helping new readers find stories similar to ours.

www.cyclingthewestcoast.com

Thank you!

Ashlin and Martin

Printed in Great Britain
by Amazon